MAKE MONEY
TRADING
LEADING
STOCKS

Debabrata (David) Das, Ph.D.

This book is dedicated to my family

PREFACE

Thank you for reading this book!

The main idea behind writing this book is to inspire novices to get conversant with the stock market. This book talks about some of the basics but frequently overlooked terminologies and calculations in trading and investing. Beginners can use this information in their virtual trading accounts. I am hoping that this book will provide motivation and food for critical thoughts to high school and university students and other newbies for a successful trading journey in their later years.

The information presented in this book can be used to make money in the stock market. The focus is more on trading the leading stocks in the leading sectors that are beating the overall market.

Many strategies, ideas, and tactics presented throughout the book can be tweaked easily to suit your own style of trading.

There are many takeaways in this book that can be directly applied to stock trading starting tomorrow.

For international readers, the FREE tools presented in this book are applicable for trading any stock market in the world.

Anybody who can surf the internet and has some basic knowledge of high school math can trade successfully using the methods discussed in this book. I hope you will find this book to be useful.

DISCLAIMER

The information presented in this book is for educational purposes only. Past performance is no guarantee of future performance. Under no circumstances, the information in this book is considered a recommendation to buy or sell any stock.

Trading stocks involves substantial risk and is not for every investor. I am not a registered financial or investment advisor. The readers should do their due diligence, research, and analysis and consult with their registered financial advisor before making any investing decisions.

Nothing in trading is guaranteed. Only trade with money that you can afford to lose. Losses are bound to happen in trading. The strategy is to keep the losses small and maximize profits. Paper trade first to test the strategy before using any real money.

All the information, data, tools, website features, etc. were accurate at the time of writing. These may change by the time you read this book.

Disclosure: I may have long or short positions in some of the stocks referenced in this book. Also, a few of the links presented in this book are affiliate links.

CONTENTS

INTRODUCTION

"Investing in yourself is the best thing you can do. If you've got talents, no one can take them from you." – Warren Buffett

Many people have asked me to share what steps I had taken to retire early. This book is a part of the series to answer those questions.

The book provides some guidance, tools, and resources so that the readers can develop their own trading strategies. Only a handful of ideas are presented here. The trading system described is strictly a rules-based trend trading system with a pre-set defined risk. The system is based on technical analysis.

The book begins by listing a few basic things that are required to commence the trading journey. An overall market trend is determined through analysis of the Index charts. The next step involves creating a watchlist of stocks constituting that Index. It is followed by highlighting the stocks which are in an uptrend.

A stock screening feature is then used to find the leading stocks within the leading sectors. A Money Management calculator is used to calculate the maximum position size (maximum number of shares to buy safely), based on risk tolerance.

Multiple time frame charts are used to discuss different Trading Plans meant for short term, medium-term, and long-term trend trading. The hyperlinks of the detailed charts have been provided below each of them. These hyperlinks can be used to view the charts on computers, tablets, or mobile devices. Several examples are used to discuss Entry Setup Criteria, Trigger Price, Stop Loss, Profit Targets, and Reward to Risk Ratios. The Reward to Risk Ratio should always be combined with the Win Rate to calculate profits.

The final chapter of the book discusses the importance of maintaining a good Trading Journal.

The tools and resources used in this book are FREE and readily available on the internet. Details on how to access these tools are shown. These FREE tools and the trading system can be utilized to trade any stock market of the world.

This book discusses only the "Long Positions," i.e., "buy low and sell high" or more precisely "buy high and sell higher." Users can adjust the settings of the charts and technical indicators, as necessary.

Appendices include a glossary, a list of useful websites, a Summary Table of the trading process, and some ideas for further research. Visit the link below to obtain FREE copies of the Money Management Calculator, Trading Journal, Summary Table and a PDF document of all Figures and Tables of this book.

- https://www.thinkandretire.com/bonus-leading-stocks/

Please do write to me if you have any questions or comments by visiting www.thinkandretire.com and clicking the "Contact" button. I will personally respond to you. I wish you all the best and success in stock trading.

CHAPTER 1: BASICS

"You can be free. You can live and work anywhere in the world. You can be independent from routine and not answer to anybody." – Alexander Elder

INTERNET CONNECTION

A reliable and secure internet connection is required to do online stock trading. The connection should be secure, strong, and stable enough so that the connection is not lost at critical moments, such as when placing the Orders.

COMPUTER

A good computer, tablet, phone and/or a mobile device is required to do research and online trading. The Trading Platforms of the Brokerage Firms have minimum system requirements. Ensure that the hardware complies with those requirements.

MINIMUM CAPITAL

There is no hard and fast rule as to how much money is needed to start trading. Every Brokerage Firm has their own minimum amounts. It is better to have a minimum of $5,000 to $10,000 in the stock trading account when getting started.

BROKERAGE ACCOUNT

An Online Trading Account with a Brokerage Firm that is registered with the regulatory organization(s), have the lowest commissions, and provides reliable services, is crucial. Interactive Brokers have lower commissions and global access. As of August 2020, their website indicates that they cover 135 markets, 33 countries, and 23 currencies. There are many good Brokerage Firms in every region. Research them and select the appropriate Online Broker that meets your requirements.

For new traders, open a "Cash Account" and NOT a "Margin Account". In "Cash Account", the trader pays the full amount for stock purchase; the Brokerage Firm does not loan money.

In "Margin Account", the Brokerage Firm can lend money for stock purchase. This is all good if the stock prices go up. However, if the stock prices go down, there is a potential risk of significant loss, even more than the invested capital.

The other important feature to look for in the Brokerage Firm is what Order Types do their trading platform offers. All of them offer the popular Order types: Market Order, Limit Order, Stop Loss Order, and Stop Limit Order. The trading platform should also have the capability of placing Bracket Order and Good Till Cancel (GTC) Order, at the least. Interactive Brokers has a great list of different Order types at the hyperlink below.

- https://www.interactivebrokers.com/en/index.php?f=4985

PAPER TRADING

For new traders, I suggest starting with a "Demo Account" (sometimes called "Practice Account" or "Virtual Trading Account"). Many Brokerage Firms offer these. TradingView.com also has the paper-trading option.

In these accounts, users receive virtual money at the beginning for buying and selling stocks. Just like a real account, the demo account shows market movements on the computer screens, so that the traders can decide if they should continue with their trade or exit the trade. In the end, the users can review their trades.

The main disadvantage of "Paper Trading" is that since there is no real money involved, the traders can take enormous risks and inflate profits. The other downside is that the stock quotes are generally not real-time.

Nevertheless, "Paper Trading" is one of the best things ever developed for traders to practice before investing real money.

CHARTING PLATFORM

This book used the FREE services of Investing.com and TradingView.com. These websites are FREE (with limitations), have many resources and user-friendly tools. They cover the major world stock markets.

These websites have the "Alerts" feature, which comes in very handy. Alerts can be set up in such a way that an email is sent to you as soon as the stocks hit a pre-set price (for example: entry price, stop loss price or profit targets), so that proper action(s) can be taken.

The FREE version of Stockcharts.com is also excellent. A list of a few more charting websites is provided in Appendix B.

CHARTS & TECHNICAL INDICATORS

A basic knowledge of chart patterns and technical indicators is needed to obtain the maximum value from this book. These patterns and indicators are generally available for FREE in almost every charting sites and platforms.

There is no need to memorize any formulas of technical indicators. Focus more on how the technical indicators are interpreted and applied on charts.

A brief description of candlesticks, chart patterns, and a few technical indicators used in this book are summarized in this section. Detailed explanations can be found in the hyperlinks below.
- https://school.stockcharts.com/doku.php?id=chart_analysis:introduction_to_candlesticks
- https://school.stockcharts.com/doku.php?id=technical_indicators

It is easy to get lost in the jungle of technical indicators. Most of the technical indicators are lagging; only a few are leading. Lagging indicators are based on past price data. Leading indicators predict where the price is headed. The technical indicators work best when stock prices are trending, not when the stock prices are choppy, or going sideways.

The technical indicators can be generally grouped together into five broad categories:
- Trend indicators
- Mean reversion indicators
- Relative strength indicators
- Momentum indicators, and
- Volume indicators.

Some of the commonly used technical indicators are: Average Directional Moving Index (ADX), Bollinger Bands, Commodity Channel Index (CCI), Directional Movement Indicator (DMI), Moving Average Convergence Divergence (MACD), Moving Averages, On Balance Volume (OBV), Parabolic Stop and Reverse (Parabolic SAR), Relative Strength Index (RSI), Stochastics, Williams %R, and many others.

Candlesticks

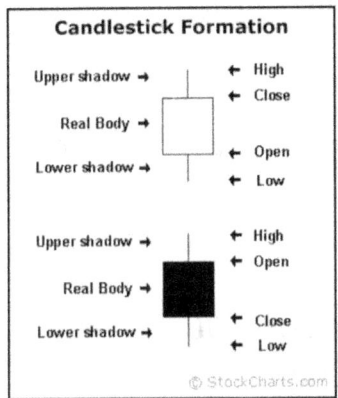

Figure 1.1 – Candlestick (Source: Stockcharts.com)

Candlestick charts are visually more appealing and easier to interpret. One candlestick provides many essential pieces of information such as stock opening price, closing price, low price, high price, either it is a bullish or a bearish day, and so on. In Figure 1.1, the top "Real Body" (white background, often colored green on charts) indicates a bullish day (stock price opened lower and closed higher). The bottom "Real Body" (black background, often colored red on charts) indicates a bearish day (stock price opened higher and closed lower).

Chart Patterns

A basic knowledge of chart patterns is useful. There are many chart patterns. An excellent summary is provided in the hyperlink below.

- https://school.stockcharts.com/doku.php?id=ch art_analysis:chart_patterns

Directional Movement Indicator (DMI)

The directions of the trend are determined by Positive Directional Indicator (+DI) and Negative Directional Indicator (–DI). These two indicators are often collectively referred to as the Directional Movement Indicator (DMI). When +DI is above the –DI, the stock price direction is generally upward. If +DI is above 25, the directional movement is stronger. Figure 1.2 explains it further.

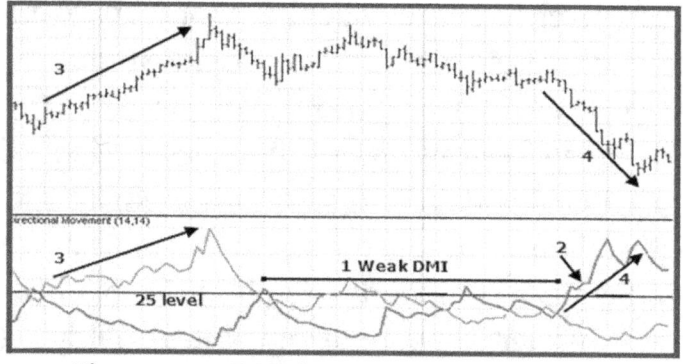

Figure 1.2 – DMI (Source: TD Ameritrade)

Average True Range (ATR) Indicator

ATR measures the stock's volatility. It is a simple but an important indicator for managing the trade.

When the volatility increases (see Figure 1.3), the candlesticks get longer and the value of ATR increases. It means, during volatile times, the stocks need more breathing room than during the less volatile times. In this book, ATR is used to determine exit points (Stop Loss and Profit Targets).

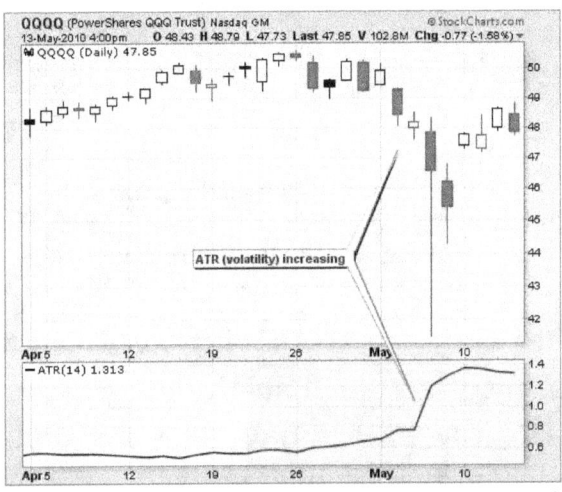

Figure 1.3 – ATR (Source: Stockcharts.com)

Moving Averages

These are the most widely used technical indicators. Moving Averages filter out the noise from the daily price movement of stocks. They are used for identifying trend directions and to determine support and resistance levels. Two moving averages are common – Exponential Moving Average (EMA) and Simple Moving Average (SMA).

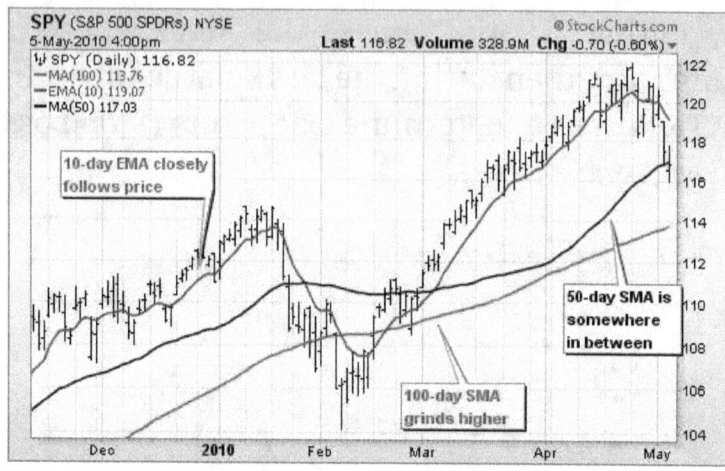

Figure 1.4 – Moving Averages (Source: Stockcharts.com)

The shorter time frame moving averages tend to be closer to the price action than the longer-term moving averages. Also, the EMA's have less lag and are more sensitive to recent price movements.

Support and Resistance

Support is the level at which demand is strong enough to stop the stock from falling any further. Think of it as the floor of a room. Drop a ball, and it bounces back. Similarly, when the stock price drops to the Support level (floor level), it bounces back UP (reverses direction).

Resistance is the level at which the supply is strong enough to stop the stock from moving higher. Think of it as the ceiling of a room. Throw a ball up in a room; it hits the ceiling and comes down. Similarly, when the stock price hits the Resistance level (ceiling), it bounces back

DOWN (reverses direction). Support and Resistance are the most discussed topics in technical analysis.

Figure 1.5 – Support and Resistance (Source: Stockcharts.com)

Figure 1.5 shows the support area with the green line (bottom line) and the resistance area with the red line (top line). Traders tend to buy when the stock price reaches the support level and sell when the stock price reaches the resistance level.

TIP

Concentrate on how the chart patterns and technical indicators are interpreted and applied on the stock price charts - no need to remember the definitions and the equations.

CHAPTER 2: OVERALL MARKET TREND

"Don't lose sight of the big picture." – John D. Rockefeller

GENERAL

Knowledge of the overall market trend is essential for successful stock trading.

OVERALL MARKET TREND

Buying stocks when the broader overall market is trending up is a good idea, for long positions. The trend will provide a tailwind for the stock prices to move higher.

For US markets, the S&P 500 Index (SPX) is the preferred choice as it covers the broader US stock market. Similar Indices are found for world stock markets (discussed in the next section).

Open a weekly chart of SPX and add two indicators: 50 SMA (Simple Moving Average) and 200 SMA.

Consider buying stocks when 50 SMA is above 200 SMA on a weekly chart of the S&P 500 Index, as shown in Figure 2.1.

For Canadian markets, the S&P TSX60 Index is my preferred choice. Like the S&P 500 Index, determine if the 50 SMA is above 200 SMA on a weekly chart of the S&P TSX 60 Index.

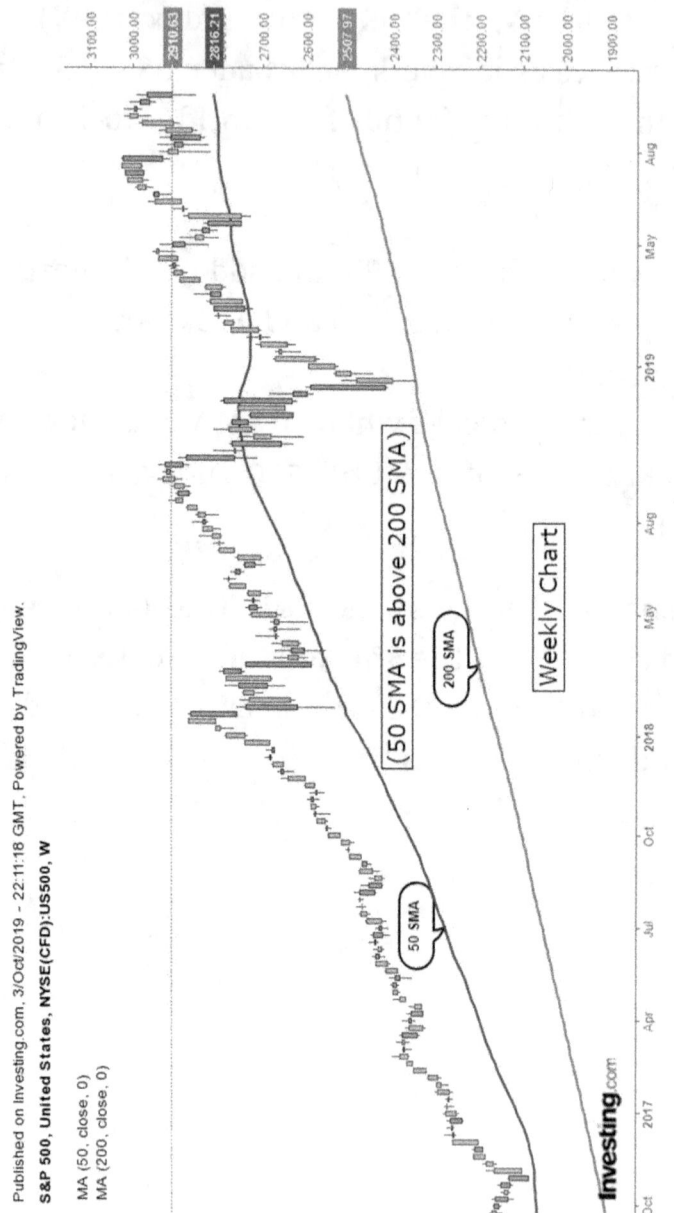

Figure 2.1 – SPX Weekly Chart (Source: Investing.com)
https://invst.ly/gm8bm

WORLD STOCK MARKET INDICES

To trade other stock markets of the world, find the appropriate Stock Market Index, which represents the broader market sentiment of that region. Some of the major stock market Indices of the world are shown in Table 2.1 below.

Location		Major Stock Market Indices
North America	Canada	S&P TSX 60
	USA	S&P 500
	USA	DOW 30
South America	Brazil	Biovespa
	Mexico	S&P/BMV IPC
Europe	England	FTSE 100
	France	CAC 40
	Germany	DAX
	Switzerland	Swiss Market Index (SMI)
Asia/Pacific	India	Nifty 50
	India	BSE Sensex
	Hong Kong	Hang Seng
	Japan	Nikkei 225
	Australia	S&P/ASX 200
Africa	South Africa	FTSE/JSE Top 40
Middle East	UAE	DFM

Table 2.1 – Major World Stock Market Indices

The hyperlinks below provide more information about major world stock market Indices.

- https://www.investing.com/indices/world-indices

- https://www.tradingview.com/markets/indices/ quotes-major/

NEXT STEP

Once it is determined that the 50 SMA is above 200 SMA on a weekly chart of the broader stock market Index (i.e., broader market is trending up on a longer time frame), the next step is to determine which stocks to select for further analysis.

TIP

Need a strong tailwind of the broader market to drive the stock prices higher. Therefore, buying stocks when the overall market is trending up is a better option.

CHAPTER 3: STOCKS WATCHLIST

"An important key to investing is to remember that stocks are not lottery tickets." – Peter Lynch

INDEX STOCKS

There are many methods of stock selection. Some people may focus on "Fundamental Analysis," while others may focus on "Technical Analysis" or on a combination of both.

For this book, the stocks belonging in the broader stock market Indices are only considered for further technical analysis. These stocks are pre-screened and have shown some merits to be included in the Indices. There are several other good stocks outside the Indices. They can also be traded profitably with proper analysis and strategies.

After selecting the Stock Market Index corresponding to the region (Chapter 2), the next task is to find stocks that constitute the Index.

In TradingView.com (hyperlink below), drill down further to the S&P 500 Index. Once you click the S&P 500 Index, notice that there is a "Components" menu above the chart. The "Components" list the names of the stocks that make up the Index. However, the components of all Indices are not listed on TradingView.com. For example, the Nifty 50 Index (hyperlink below) components are not provided in TradingView.com.

- https://www.tradingview.com/markets/indices/quotes-major/
- https://www.tradingview.com/symbols/NSE-NIFTY/

The reverse is true for Investing.com. The "Components" are not provided for S&P 500 Index, but they are provided for Nifty 50 Index. In Investing.com, just click "Add to Portfolio" button and add stocks to the Watchlist (labelled as "portfolio" in Investing.com).

If the "Components" (stocks) which comprise the Index are not provided at these websites, a quick internet search can provide the information.

S&P 500 STOCKS (US)

The S&P 500 (SPX) is a stock market Index that measures the performance of stocks of 500 large companies listed on stock exchanges in the United States. It is a market-capitalization-weighted Index of the 500 largest U.S. publicly traded companies. The Index is widely regarded as the best gauge of large-cap U.S. equities.

The list of S&P 500 stocks is available online or by visiting the first hyperlink below.

- https://www.tradingview.com/symbols/SPX/components/

S&P TSX 60 STOCKS (CANADA)

The S&P/TSX 60 Index is a stock market index of 60 large companies listed on the Toronto Stock Exchange (as measured by float adjusted market capitalization weighted). For the latest list of S&P TSX 60 Stocks, please visit the first hyperlink below.

- https://web.tmxmoney.com/indices.php?section=tsx&index=^TX60#indexInfo

WORLD INDICES

The World Indices can be found from the links below:
- https://www.investing.com/indices/world-indices
- https://www.tradingview.com/markets/indices/quotes-major/

The objective is to find the appropriate broader market stock Index of the region (described in Chapter 2) and then obtain the names of the stocks that constitute that Index.

WATCHLIST (INDEX STOCKS)

Create a watchlist of all the stocks which constitute the Index. The advantage of using a watchlist is that by just clicking the stock symbol, the charts are displayed simultaneously. It eliminates the need to type the stock symbol every time.

Watchlists can be created easily using Investing.com or TradingView.com. In Investing.com, it is labelled as "portfolio" instead of "watchlist". Multiple watchlists can be created in the FREE version of Investing.com. The

FREE version of TradingView.com is restricted to only one watchlist. However, TradingView.com has the advantage of color coding the stock symbols (like a bookmark or a flag) of interest for future references.

STRONG TRENDING STOCKS

Trading strong trending stocks has its advantages. Strong up trending stocks demonstrate higher highs and higher lows as illustrated in Figure 3.1. The reverse is true for down trending stocks. Figure 3.1 illustrates a stock chart with smooth trending patterns (downtrend on the left, and uptrend on the right). For this book, the focus is only on the uptrend portion of the charts.

Only a few stocks show smooth trends like the one shown in Figure 3.1. It is easier to trade stocks which demonstrate smooth trending patterns.

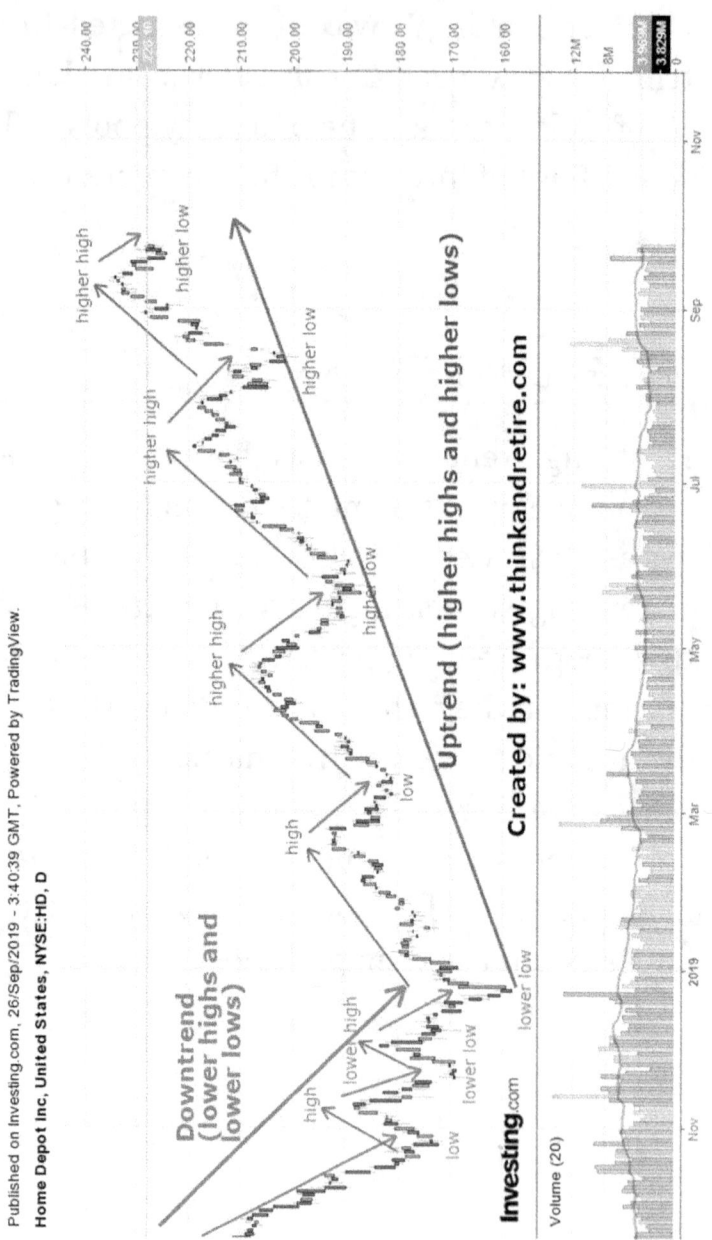

Figure 3.1 – Trending Patterns (Source: Investing.com)
https://invst.ly/dmdlo

FOCUS ON SMOOTH TRENDING STOCKS

Once the stocks are added to the Watchlist, click through the stock symbols, and visually check the weekly charts first. Flag or bookmark the stock symbols whose weekly charts have a smooth trending pattern and meet the following criteria (on a weekly chart):

- The 50 SMA is above 200 SMA, and
- The price action has higher highs and higher lows.

A few chart examples, meeting the above criteria are shown in the next four figures (Figures 3.2 to 3.5).

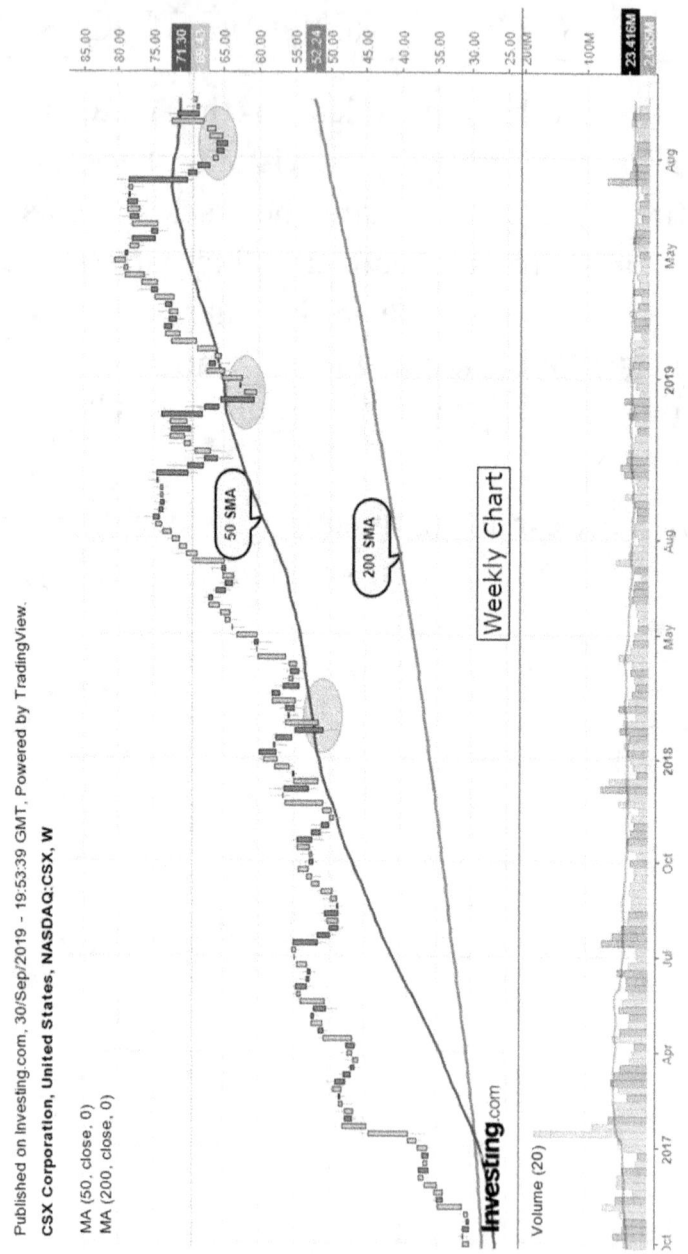

Figure 3.2 – Trending Stock Example 1 (Source: Investing.com)
https://invst.ly/fe56t

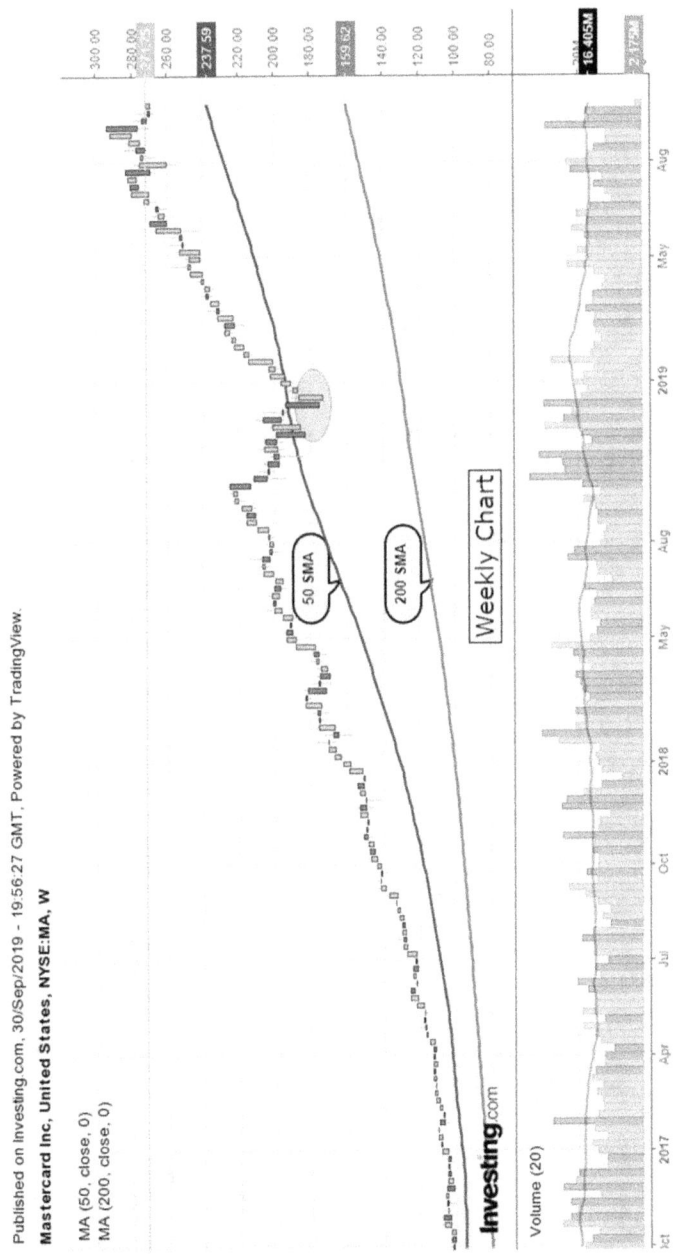

Figure 3.3 –Trending Stock Example 2 (Source: Investing.com)
https://invst.ly/fe5y0

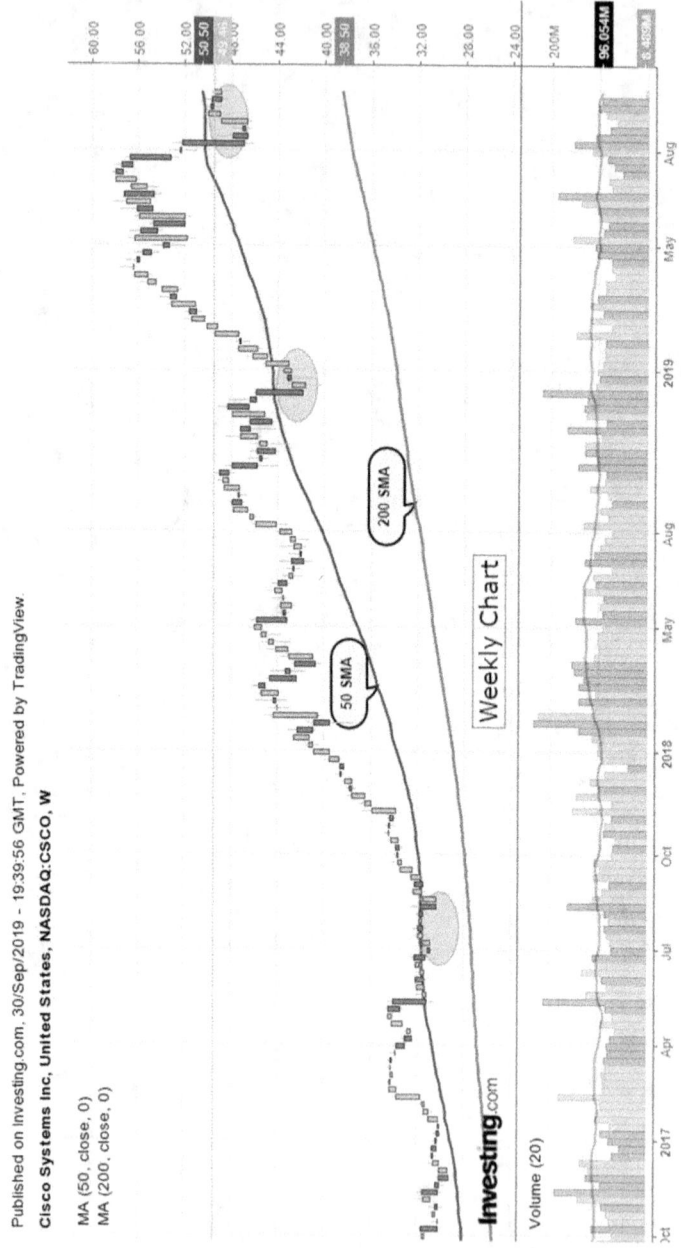

Figure 3.4 –Trending Stock Example 3 (Source: Investing.com)
https://invst.ly/fe20t

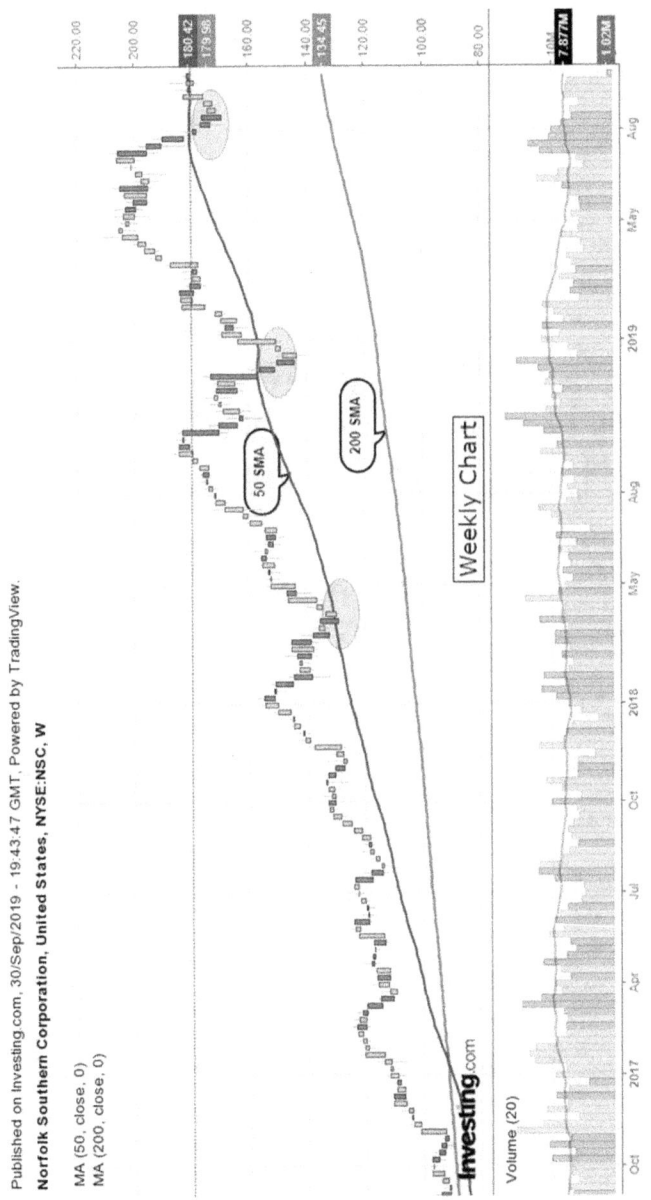

Figure 3.5 –Trending Stock Example 4 (Source: Investing.com)
https://invst.ly/fe2uy

TIP

Stocks are periodically added and deleted from the Stock Indices. Check the Indices quarterly to see which stocks have been deleted from or added to the Indices. Then update the Watchlist accordingly.

CHAPTER 4: LEADING SECTORS AND LEADING STOCKS

"Trade the market in front of you, not the one you want." – Scott Redler

MEANING

There are about 500 stocks in the S&P 500 Index. The obvious question is which stocks to choose? Although there are no guarantees in the stock market, it makes perfect sense to select the stocks which have a higher probability of price escalation. The concept is the same as a horse race, where people bet on high-performance horses, which have a history of winning in the past.

There are many methods of stock selection. As mentioned earlier, some traders use fundamental analysis; others use technical analysis or a combination of both.

Trading stocks that are outperforming the broader stock market have a higher probability of success. The methodology used in this book will be predominantly based on technical analysis and applying the following rules in the selection process:

- Does the stock belong to one of the Leading Sectors?
- Is the stock one of the Leading Stocks in the Leading Sector? and
- Is the stock outperforming the broader stock market?

The concept of "Relative Strength" will briefly be discussed next to explain the above.

RELATIVE STRENGTH

"Relative Strength" measures the performance of one security against another, or more commonly, against a benchmark index, such as the S&P 500 Index (SPX). The security can be a stock, a sector, or an industry. We can compare stock vs. stock, stock vs. sector, stock vs. SPX, sector vs. sector, sector vs. SPX, and so on. This exercise determines if a stock or a sector or an industry is outperforming its peers. "Relative Strength" should not be confused with the "Relative Strength Index" (RSI) indicator. We are using "Relative Strength" in this book and NOT the "RSI" indicator. RSI is a momentum oscillator, whereas the Relative Strength looks at a relationship between two investments.

There are a few methods of calculating Relative Strength. This book will show two methods. The first method is to compare the percentage change in stock price by the percentage change in Index (SPX) price within the same time frame. The second method is to divide the stock price by the Index price and plotting the result. This chapter will use the first method.

LEADING SECTORS

Just because the overall market is trending higher does not mean all the sectors are performing well. Some sectors will perform better than the others.

TradingView.com divides the US stock market into 11 Sectors (hyperlink at the end of this paragraph). Some may divide the stock market into 12 Sectors. The objective in this step is to find the Leading Sectors first and then find the Leading Stocks within those Leading Sectors.

- https://www.tradingview.com/markets/indices/quotes–snp/

From the TradingView.com website, the performance data of the Sectors and the SPX for different timeframes are noted. The Sectors are first sorted by "Weekly Performance". After sorting the results for one week, one month, three months, six months, and one-year timeframes, the summary data is tabulated in Table 4.1.

Top 5 Leading Sectors – different timeframes, vs S&P 500 (SPX)				
1w perf (%)	1m perf (%)	3m perf (%)	6m perf (%)	1y perf (%)
Technology (1.16)	Utilities (2.06)	Utilities (4.53)	Non-cyclicals(8.26)	Utilities (21.03)
Healthcare (0.37)	Telecom (1.64)	Telecom (1.98)	Utilities (8.05)	Noncyclical(15.08)
Utilities (0.19)	Financials (0.68)	Technology (1.89)	Technology (4.30)	Technology (9.78)
Telecom (0.16)	Non-cyclical(-0.02)	Non-cyclicals(0.96)	Cyclicals (2.73)	Cyclicals (6.70)
Non-cyclical(0.05)	Energy (-0.38)	Industrial (-0.70)	Telecom (2.71)	Telecom (5.45)
SPX (-0.33)	SPX (-0.81)	SPX (-0.80)	SPX (2.05)	SPX (1.74)
Note: Information correct as of Oct 4, 2019 after market close				

Table 4.1 – Top 5 Leading Sectors (as of Oct 4, 2019)

Table 4.1 shows that all the Top 5 Leading Sectors performed better than the broader stock market.

The information from Table 4.1 is now used to find out which sectors showed up the most in different timeframes, as shown in Table 4.2.

Common Leading Sectors – different timeframes	
Time Frames	Common Sectors
1wk + 1m + 3m	Utilities, Telecommunications, Non-cyclicals
1m + 3m + 6m	Utilities, Telecommunications, Non-cyclicals
3m + 6m + 1yr	Utilities, Telecommunications, Non-cyclicals, Technology
6m + 1yr	Utilities, Telecommunications, Non-cyclicals, Technology, Cyclicals
Note: Information correct as of Oct 4, 2019 after market close	

Table 4.2 – Common Leading Sectors (as of Oct 4, 2019)

Table 4.2 indicates the common Leading Sectors in the short term, medium-term, and on a long-term basis.

The comparison of "Consumer Cyclicals" and "Consumer Non-Cyclicals" (also called "Consumer Staples") deserves a bit more discussion.

The "Consumer Cyclicals" (also called "Consumer Discretionary") Sector includes industries that offer non-essential products and services, such as automobiles, entertainment, leisure, apparel, home furnishings, casinos and gaming and so on. When the economy is strong, "Consumer Cyclicals" (Consumer Discretionary) Sector is strong.

On the other hand, the "Consumer Non-Cyclicals" (also called as "Consumer Staples") Sector includes industries related to food (processing, retail, and distribution), non-alcoholic beverages, fishing and farming, household products, personal products and services, drug retailers, breweries, distillers, wineries, and tobacco. These items are considered essentials and will be consumed, no matter if the economy is strong or weak. This sector is generally stable throughout the year.

Table 4.2 indicates that "Consumer Cyclicals" (Consumer Discretionary) Sector did not show up as Top 5 Leading Sectors for one week, one month, and three months' timeframes. It means that the general economy has been relatively weaker in recent months, compared to a year ago.

The next step will be to find the Leading Stocks in the Leading Sectors.

LEADING STOCKS

This section will discuss how to pick the Leading Stocks in the Leading Sectors, such as Utilities, Telecommunications, and Non-Cyclicals.

Leading Stocks in Utilities Sector

Use the "Stock Screener" feature of TradingView.com (https://www.tradingview.com/screener/) and scan for top stocks in the Utilities Sector. The following eight filter criteria were used in the selection process:

- **Symbol type:** only interested in the common stocks,
- **Average Volume:** need liquidity, so pick stocks which trades more than 500K/day on average (30 days average chosen), thereby avoiding stocks which trade at low volumes per day,
- **Exchange:** interested in stocks trading on reputed exchanges,
- **Index:** interested in the S&P 500 Index stocks (for US, use similar indices for other markets),
- **Last (Price):** need the stock price to be over $10. Not interested in low-priced or penny stocks,
- **Market Capitalization:** interested in stocks which are midcap (+2B) and higher [including (large-cap (+10B) and mega-cap (+200B)],
- **Sector:** focussed on the Utilities Sector as it was one of the strongest Sectors determined earlier, and
- **Simple Moving Average (SMA 50):** want the stock price to be at or above the 50 SMA, used as the reference line for going long.

Similar scanning can be done for other stock markets of the world by changing the "Country" and the Index. For other countries, some adjustments may be needed for some of the filters, such as average volume, stock price, and market cap values.

Twenty-five matches (stocks) were found that met the selection criteria on the search day (after market closed on Oct 4, 2019). Go to the "Performance" tab and adjust the columns, so that the performances for one week, one month, three months, and so on, can be compared (same as Sectors). The SPX and Sector performance data were also obtained.

After sorting the results for different timeframes, the summary data showing the top 5 Utilities stocks meeting the screening criteria is shown in Table 4.3.

Top 5 Utilities Stocks – different timeframes vs SPX & Utilities Sector				
1w perf (%)	1m perf (%)	3m perf (%)	6m perf (%)	1y perf (%)
SRE (1.90)	NEE (6.27)	ETR (13.8)	ETR (25.72)	ETR (46.27)
CMS (1.42)	EIX (6.00)	WEC (12.65)	NEE (22.89)	SO (44.37)
WEC (1.28)	D (5.51)	NEE (11.70)	WEC (22.83)	AWK (43.47)
AWK (1.24)	CNP (4.50)	ES (11.12)	ES (20.44)	WEC (42.81)
ETR (1.08)	ES (4.36)	FE (10.75)	SO (20.14)	ES (39.11)
SPX (-0.33)	SPX (-0.81)	SPX (-0.80)	SPX (2.05)	SPX (1.74)
Utilities Sec. (0.19)	Utilities Sec (2.06)	Utilities Sec. (4.53)	Utilities Sec. (8.05)	Utilities Sec.(21.03)
Note: Information correct as of Oct 4, 2019 after market close. This is NOT a recommendation to buy or sell any stock.				

Table 4.3 – Top 5 Utilities Stocks (as of Oct 4, 2019)

Table 4.3 indicates that all the Top 5 Stocks meeting the selection criteria in the Utilities Sector performed better than the broader stock market and the Sector itself.

Leading Stocks in the Telecommunications Sector

A similar screening process was adopted with one change: changed the Sector to Telecommunications. The SPX and the Sector performance data were also obtained.

The data was then sorted for other time frames. The table below shows the top Telecommunications stocks (only 2 were found) meeting the screening criteria for different timeframes.

Top Telecommunications Stocks – different timeframes vs SPX & Sector				
1w perf (%)	1m perf (%)	3m perf (%)	6m perf (%)	1y perf (%)
T (0.21)	T (4.51)	T (9.52)	T (15.95)	T (9.94)
VZ (-0.66)	VZ (2.24)	VZ (3.47)	VZ (1.37)	VZ (8.87)
SPX (-0.33)	SPX (-0.81)	SPX (-0.80)	SPX (2.05)	SPX (1.74)
Sector (0.16)	Sector (1.64)	Sector (1.98)	Sector (2.71)	Sector (5.45)
VZ Performed below SPX and the Telecom Sector				
Note: Information correct as of Oct 4, 2019 after market close.				
This is NOT a recommendation to buy or sell any stock.				

Table 4.4 – Top Telecommunications Stocks (as of Oct 4, 2019)

Table 4.4 indicates that only one stock "T" met the selection criteria in the Telecommunications Sector and performed better than the broader stock market and the Sector itself.

Leading Stocks in Consumer Non-Cyclicals Sector

A screening was conducted for the Consumer Non-Cyclicals Sector after the market closed on Oct 4, 2019. The SPX and the Sector performance data were also obtained.

After sorting through the results further for one week, one month, three months, six months and, one-year timeframes, the summary table showing the top 5 Non-Cyclicals' stocks meeting the screening criteria for different timeframes is presented in Table 4.5.

Top 5 Non-cyclicals Stocks – different timeframes vs SPX & Sector				
1w perf (%)	1m perf (%)	3m perf (%)	6m perf (%)	1y perf (%)
MKC (7.76)	PM (8.80)	CPB (14.07)	HSY (35.94)	HSY (53.32)
PM (4.19)	TAP (6.49)	KR (13.72)	CPB (23.73)	PG (51.37)
PEP (3.45)	CPB (6.10)	HSY (13.65)	EL (21.19)	EL (44.48)
HSY (2.43)	SYY (5.07)	K (13.35)	PG (19.63)	MDLZ (32.12)
MDLZ (1.07)	ADM (4.45)	BF.B (11.33)	WMT (19.56)	PEP (31.58)
SPX (-0.33)	SPX (-0.81)	SPX (-0.80)	SPX (2.05)	SPX (1.74)
Sector (0.05)	Sector (-0.02)	Sector (0.96)	Sector (8.26)	Sector (15.08)
Note: Information correct as of Oct 4, 2019 after market close. This is NOT a recommendation to buy or sell any stock.				

Table 4.5 – Top 5 Non-Cyclicals' Stocks (as of Oct 4, 2019)

Table 4.5 indicates that all the Top 5 Stocks meeting the selection criteria in the Non-Cyclicals Sector performed better than the broader stock market and the Sector itself.

OTHER FILTERING OPTIONS

So far, the discussions were focused on a systematic approach to select leading stocks. Another way to start researching is to look for stocks that are making "52 weeks highs" or "New All–Time Highs." These stocks have a higher probability of beating the broader stock market. Also, if these stocks belong to any of the leading Sectors, then the probability increases further for stock price appreciation (no guarantees though!).

TradingView.com and many other websites have "52 Week High" and "New All Time–High" listings of stocks.

However, it is always a good idea to do your own research before rushing to buy any stock.

TOUCH OF FUNDAMENTALS

We now have a list of leading stocks in leading sectors meeting the rigorous selection criteria. This list may appear long. Too many stocks to choose from. The stock list can then be further narrowed down.

Although the Fundamental Analysis of a stock is beyond the scope of this book, apply one filter by ensuring that the stocks have a minimum Return on Equity (ROE) of 15%. This information is readily available in TradingView.com (under Fundamentals tab) or any other financial websites (like Yahoo Finance, MSN Money, etc.).

NEXT STEP

Now we have a list of top-performing stocks in top-performing Sectors, beating the broader stock market. It does not mean that we are ready to buy these stocks tomorrow. Various "Entry Setup" Criteria (sometimes called "Setups") need to be met, which will be discussed in Chapter 6.

In Chapter 5, the Money Management technique is discussed. This chapter explains how to manage risks (losses) before buying a stock.

TIP

No matter what happens with the economy, people will consume products and services, which are in the "Consumer Non-Cyclicals" Sector (also termed as "Consumer Staples"). It is generally considered a stable Sector.

CHAPTER 5: MONEY MANAGEMENT

"Successful investing is about managing risk, not avoiding it." – Benjamin Graham

MEANING

The main objectives of the Money Management process include deciding on how much loss a trader can safely take, how much capital to invest, and how many shares to buy. We have no control over the markets, but we have full control over our invested capital. An effective money management process will be a crucial factor in differentiating between capital preservation and capital appreciation.

Before we get into the calculations, let me introduce the concepts of "Stop Loss", "Account Risk," and "Trade Risk."

STOP LOSS

Stop Loss is an advance order to sell a stock when it reaches a pre-set price limit.

Stop Loss is a process of controlling risk. The challenge is to determine at what price point to take a loss. If the stop loss is too tight, the stock price may just hit the stop loss and reverse back up. It can be very frustrating when that happens. On the contrary, if the stop loss is too wide, the loss may increase significantly.

There are many methods of Stop Loss placement, as indicated below:
- Fixed $ amount
- Fixed % amount
- Swing low
- Day's low
- Fixed Support
- Dynamic Support (like moving averages)
- Average True Range (ATR), and many others.

Chapter 6 has many examples of Stop Loss use.

ACCOUNT RISK

Conservative traders can cap the risk at 1% of invested capital (Account Size). If the trading account is $10,000, the Account Risk is $100. For a $5,000 account, the Account Risk is $50, and so on. The percentage can be increased based on your risk tolerance level.

TRADE RISK

Trade risk is the potential loss amount per share. If the stock buy price is $25/share, and the stop loss is at $24/share, then the trade risk is $1/share. If the stock buy price is $25/share, and the stop loss is at $23/share, then the trade risk is $2/share, and so on.

A Stop Loss Order does not guarantee the specified exit price in a volatile market or during the overnight gaps. A lower Account Risk strategy can save from those big moves in the stock price.

OPTIMAL POSITION SIZE (CASH ACCOUNT, NON-LEVERAGED)

For new traders, opening a "Cash" Account with a Discount Brokerage Firm is a better option. It means that if all the trades go in the reverse direction, the loss is limited to the maximum amount of the Account Size (Invested Capital).

Based on the account size, risk tolerance level, and the trade risk, the Optimal Position Size can be calculated as shown in Table 5.1. Commission costs are kept zero to keep the calculations simple.

Cash Account - Money Management Calculator for Position Sizing				
Description	Option 1	Option 2	Option 3	Option 4
Capital (Account Size)	$10,000	$10,000	$10,000	$10,000
% Risk on Capital (Account Size)	1%	1%	1%	1%
Account Risk	$100.00	$100.00	$100.00	$100.00
Entry Price/Share	$25.00	$25.00	$25.00	$25.00
Stop Loss Price/Share	$24.50	$24.00	$23.50	$23.00
Trade Risk/Share	$0.50	$1.00	$1.50	$2.00
Commission (assumed zero)	$0.00	$0.00	$0.00	$0.00
Maximum Shares that can be bought	400	400	400	400
Risk Adjusted Maximum Trade Size	200	100	66	50
Optimal Position Size	200	100	66	50
Actual Account Risk	$100.00	$100.00	$99.00	$100.00
Total Cost of the Trade	$5,000.00	$2,500.00	$1,650.00	$1,250.00

Table 5.1 – Money Management Calculator

Table 5.1 shows that the Account Size is $10,000, and the Account Risk is $100. The Optimal Position Size (maximum number of shares to buy) is different depending on Trade Risk (stop loss) per share.

If there is no cap on the risk amount, a maximum of 400 shares of $25 stock could have been purchased in a $10,000 Cash account ($10,000 divided by $25).

There is a potential of a significant loss in this scenario, even up to the invested capital of $10,000. If the company goes bankrupt, or if the stock price goes down to $0 or if the stock is de-listed from the exchange for any reason, the entire account will be wiped out.

However, if the Account Risk is capped to 1% (Account risk: $100), 200 shares can be purchased in Option 1 (trade risk $0.50/share), or 100 shares in Option 2 (trade risk $1.00/share), or 66 shares in Option 3 (trade risk $1.50/share), or 50 shares in Option 4 (trade risk $2.00/share). For all these options, there is an unlimited profit potential, and the maximum risk is capped. The stock price can still go to zero, but your account is not wiped out, thereby limiting the risk.

As noted in Table 5.1, for tighter stops ($0.50 in Option 1), relatively more shares can be purchased. However, there is a higher probability that the Stop Loss price is hit, and the shares are sold at the Stop Loss price.

Conversely, for wider stops ($2.00 in Option 4), relatively lower number of shares can be purchased. There is a lower probability that the Stop Loss price is hit, and we are still in the trade.

The total cost of the trade decreases as the number of shares bought is reduced with wider stops.

OPTIMAL POSITION SIZE (MARGIN ACCOUNT, LEVERAGED)

"Margin" account is a practice of borrowing money from the Brokerage Firm to buy stocks. Brokerage Firms will use the shares as collateral and will charge interest on the borrowed money. In "Margin" accounts, both the losses and the gains are magnified. There are a few advantages of "Margin" accounts; however, in these types of accounts, there is a possibility of losing more money than the Invested Capital. For beginners, a margin account is not a good idea.

TIP

Questions may arise as to which variable to adjust if the Account Risk is kept constant (say 1% in this example): a) position size, or b) the stop loss? If the stop loss is determined based on the volatility of the market (that we have less control over), it makes more sense to adjust the "position size".

CHAPTER 6: TRADING PLAN

"It's not whether you're right or wrong, but how much money you make when you're right and how much you lose when you're wrong." – George Soros

BE INFORMED

The methodology discussed in this book is not based on trading news events. However, it is always a good practice to stay informed about what is happening in the stock market.

Economic Calendars include the schedule of the upcoming "High Impact" news events, such as announcements on: Interest Rates, Building Permits,

Employment Cost Index, Non-Farm Payroll (NFP), Monetary Policy meetings, Federal Open Market Committee (FOMC) meetings, Unemployment Rate and Jobs Report, GDP growth, Inflation data – Consumer Price/Produce Price Indexes (CPI and PPI), Retail Sales, Crude Oil Inventories and so on. These news events can affect the stock market and the stock price. A list of websites showing the economic calendars are in Appendix B.

If a trader plans to buy a stock, it is better to enter a new trade after the announcement of the "High Impact" news. On the other hand, if the trader has an open position and trading for the short term, either sell the shares before the "High Impact News" or closely monitor the stock price during the event.

"Earnings Release" dates are also critical, as the stock prices become more volatile during that time. When entering a short-term trade, ensure that there are no earnings release dates (of the company) in the next 3 to 4 weeks. A list of earnings calendar websites is in Appendix B.

TradingView.com has the features where "Show Economic Events" and "Show Earnings" can be added on the charts. This can come in very handy.

AVERAGE TRUE RANGE (ATR)

Average True Range (ATR) is one of my favorite indicators to measure volatility. ATR has many uses. For this book, a 14-period ATR is used for calculating the Stop Loss price.

With the ATR method, the market will decide where to place the Stop Loss, rather than choosing an arbitrary value.

There are no set rules as to what multiples of ATR to use. It depends on how tight the traders want their Stop Loss (Trade Risk) to be. The stock prices will fluctuate; it is a normal behavior. Some traders are more conservative than the others.

For short term trend trading, I use "1.5*ATR" as the Stop Loss. Therefore, the Stop Loss Price is placed at "Buy Price − 1.5*ATR".

Example: If the purchase price of a stock is $100/share, and the ATR is $4, the Stop Loss Price will be at $94

(=\$100 − 1.5*\$4). It means, after buying, if the stock price touches or falls below \$94, the broker will sell the stock at \$94, therefore limiting the loss to \$6 per share.

A Stop Loss Order does not guarantee the specified exit price in a volatile market or during the overnight gaps. In such situations, it is better to place a Stop Loss Order rather than a Stop Loss Limit Order. In normal circumstances, Stop Loss Limit Order will fill the Order at the pre-set limit. Differences between Stop Loss and Stop Loss Limit Order are in the hyperlink below:

- https://www.thestreet.com/story/10273105/1/ask-thestreet-limits-and-losses.html

For the medium term, I use "3*ATR" as the Initial Stop Loss. So, the Stop Loss Price is at "Buy Price − 3*ATR". For the longer-term, I use a 6 to 8*ATR as the Stop Loss.

TRADING PLAN

The Trading Plan will consist of ALL the following pieces of information before purchasing a stock:

- Entry Setups
- Trigger Price
- Stop Loss Price, and
- Profit Target(s)

The sections below will discuss three different Trading Plans: for short term, medium-term, and long-term trend trading. This book will only discuss the Long Positions.

There are no right ways or wrong ways of entering or exiting a trade. If a strategy is making consistent profitable trades, that is the winning strategy.

There are unlimited number of Setups for Entry. The easiest way to find them is through stock scanning. The scan results are the starting point (narrows down the number of stocks) for further analysis.

Many websites offer pre-defined Scans, such as Stockcharts.com. Their website is limited to stocks trading in the US, Canada, London, and Indian stock exchanges. Another good site in Finviz.com for scanning of US stocks. Chartmill.com offers similar services, but for the US, Canada, London, and many European stock exchanges. Several other websites offer related services. The hyperlinks of the above 3 websites are as follows:
- https://stockcharts.com/def/servlet/SC.scan
- https://finviz.com/screener.ashx
- https://www.chartmill.com/stock/stock-screener?affl=84995

The search results or the shortlist of stocks from the above websites should be noted for further analysis. These stocks should not be purchased immediately. The technical indicators work best when stock prices are trending, not when the stock prices are choppy. So, we need to ensure that: a) the overall market is trending up, and b) the long-term weekly chart of the stock is trending up with higher highs and higher lows. Also, ensure that the stocks meet the following criteria:

- **Average Volume:** need liquidity, so pick stocks which trades more than 500K/day on average (of 30 days), thereby avoiding stocks which trade at low volumes per day,
- **Exchange:** interested in stocks trading at reputed exchanges,
- **Index:** interested in S&P 500 Index stocks (for US, use similar indices for other markets),
- **Last (Price):** need the stock price to be over $10. Not interested in low-priced or penny stocks,
- **Market Capitalization:** interested in stocks which are midcap (+2B) and higher [including (large-cap (+10B) and mega-cap (+200B)],
- **Sector:** focus on the Leading Sectors, and
- **Simple Moving Average (SMA 50):** want the stock price to be at or above the 50 SMA.

We now have a shortlist of stocks which have been through stringent selection criteria. Proper Setups are required for entering the trade. As indicated earlier, there are unlimited number of Setups for Entry. I will focus on a few of them in the examples to follow. Several other setups are listed in Appendix E for further research. Traders should develop their own strategies based on their trading style and objectives.

TRADING PLAN – SHORT TERM TREND TRADING

For short term trend trading, I will use a fixed 2:1 Reward to Risk Ratio for managing the trade.

ENTRY SETUP CRITERIA

I am discussing one of my favorite Setups in this section. The Setup will occur when the Positive Directional Indicator (+DI) crosses above 25 on the daily stock chart if the other conditions are met as noted below. 14 period DI indicator is used for all the examples.

Condition 1: On the weekly chart of the S&P 500 Index (SPX) (for US, use similar indices for other markets):
- Price pattern is smooth and trending up,
- 50 SMA is above 200 SMA, and
- SPX price is above 50 SMA

Condition 2: On the weekly stock chart:

- Price pattern is smooth and trending up,
- 50 SMA is above 200 SMA, and
- Positive Directional Indicator (+DI) is above Negative Directional Indicator (−DI)

Condition 3: On the daily stock chart:

- Positive Directional Indicator (+DI) crossed above 25,
- Price is above 50 SMA or just crossed above 50 SMA, and
- No earnings announcements within the next 3 to 4 weeks

How to determine when +DI crossed above 25 on the daily chart? It can be done by looking at the chart itself. It can also be automated by adding the following condition to the stock screener. In TradingView.com it will be (https://www.tradingview.com/screener/):

- Positive Directional Indicator (14) −> Crosses Up −> 25

TRIGGER PRICE

Trigger Price is the price where the Buy/Sell Orders become active for execution. The following paragraphs will explain its application for Buy Orders.

Say, on Day 1, all the three conditions of Entry Setup are met, and the trader wants to buy shares of a company. After the market closes on Day 1 or before opening the next trading day (say Day 2), place a Buy Stop Limit Day Order with the Limit Price equal to the last closing price (Day 1 closing price), or any other desired price point. The closing price is used for discussions because it is directly obtained from the stock chart and is not arbitrarily chosen.

It means that on Day 2, for the Buy Order to be executed anytime during the day, the stock price must touch the Limit Price. If this happens, the Entry Price or the Buy Price becomes the Trigger Price, and the Buy Order is executed.

On the other hand, if on Day 2, the stock opens lower, remains lower throughout the day, and never touches the Limit Price, the Buy Order will not be executed. The Buy Order will be void automatically at the end of the trading day.

Similarly, on Day 2, if the stock price opens higher, remains higher throughout the day, and never touches the Limit Price, the Buy Order will not be executed. The

Buy Order will be void automatically at the end of the trading day.

For Buy Orders, the Trigger Price gives the trader an opportunity to only buy shares if the price trend is continuing higher. At the same time, it keeps the Buy price at check (i.e., not pay too much for the share). The reverse is true for Sell Orders.

STOP LOSS PRICE

For short term trend trading, I use 1.5*ATR as the Stop Loss, also referred to as Trade Risk per share. Therefore, the Stop Loss Price = Buy Price – 1.5*ATR.

PROFIT TARGET

For short term trading, I will have a fixed Profit Target of 2 times the Trade Risk (or Stop Loss).

Our Trade Risk was 1.5*ATR. Therefore, the Profit Target = Buy Price + 2*Stop Loss = Buy Price + 3*ATR.

SHORT TERM TREND TRADING EXAMPLES

Two short term trading examples are presented. Once all the three conditions are met, the stock closing price and the ATR value are recorded for the day. Money Management calculator is then used to obtain the

Optimal Position Sizing info (maximum number of shares that can be purchased safely).

Investing.com and TradingView.com charts have a built-in "Long Position" feature, which can automatically calculate the maximum number of shares to buy, based on pre-set Account Size and Account Risk tolerance level. This "Long Position" tool is displayed to the left of the charts in TradingView.com and Investing.com, and it looks like the figure below.

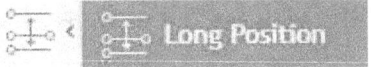

Figure 6.1 – "Long Position" Tool (Source: TradingView.com)

Open the "Settings" on the above tool. Change the Account Size and the Account Risk percentage according to your situation. For the examples shown below, the Account Size is set to $10,000 and the Account Risk to 1%.

EXAMPLE 1: HOME DEPOT (HD)

The Setup will occur when the Positive Directional Indicator (+DI) crosses above 25 on the daily chart.

On Aug 20, 2019, all the three conditions were met for this Home Depot (HD) trade example (see Figures 6.2 and 6.3).

Condition 1: On the weekly chart of SPX, the price chart was smooth and trending up, 50 SMA is above 200 SMA, and SPX price was above 50 SMA (Figure 6.2).

Condition 2: On the weekly chart of Home Depot (HD), the price chart was smooth and trending up, 50 SMA was above 200 SMA, and +DI was above –DI (Figure 6.3).

Condition 3: On Aug 20, 2019, +DI crossed above 25 on the daily chart. The stock price was also above 50 SMA (Figure 6.3). The earnings were reported before the market open on Aug 20, 2019, so the next earnings will be reported about three months later.

The closing price of the stock on Aug 20, 2019, was $217.09, and ATR was 4.56. Hence, the Trade Risk/share (Stop Loss) = 1.5*ATR = 1.5*$4.56 = $6.84, say $6.85. Stop Loss Price will be set at $210.24 (= $217.09 – $6.85). Profit Target = Buy Price + 2*Stop Loss = $230.79 (= $217.09 + 2*$6.85).

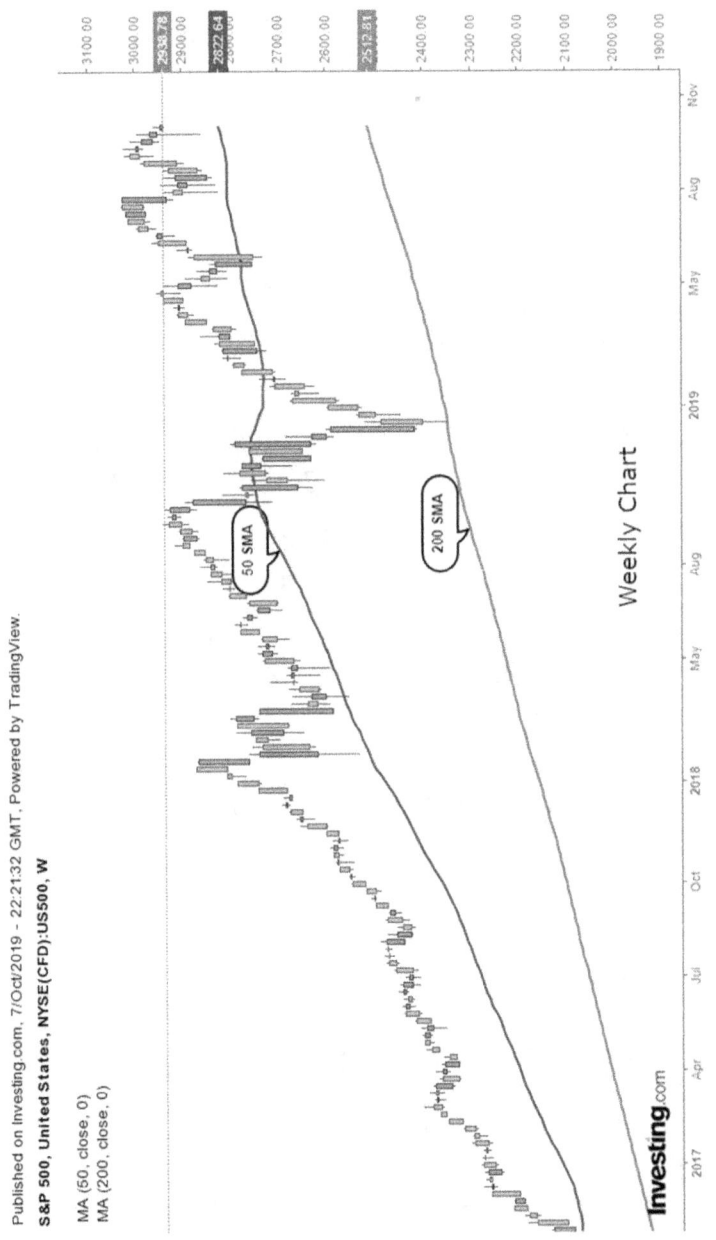

Figure 6.2 – SPX Weekly Chart (Source: Investing.com)
https://invst.ly/i6rbb

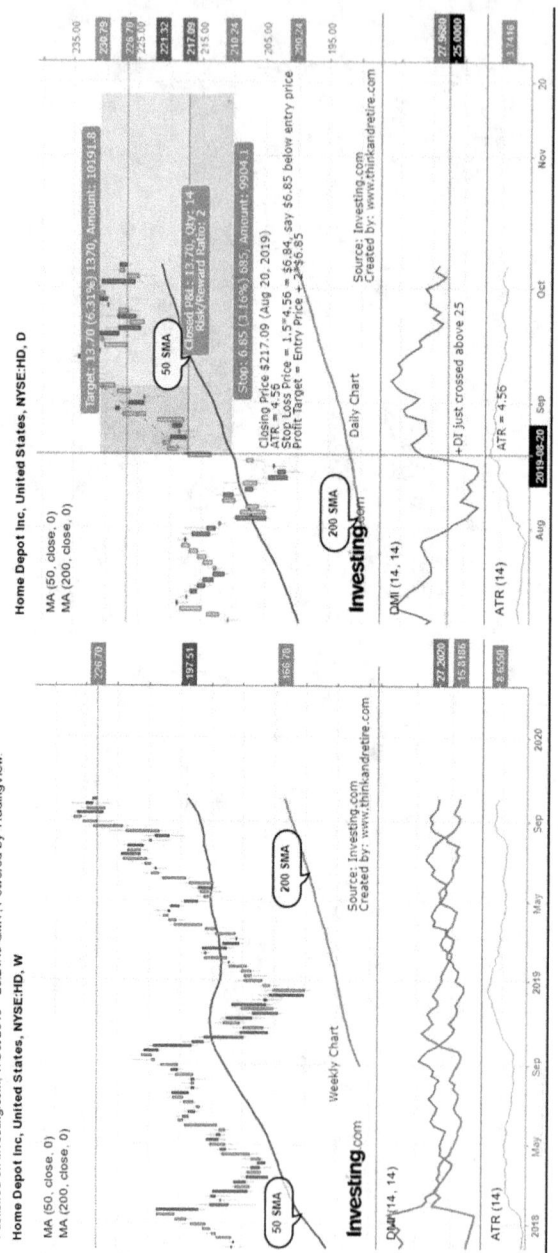

Figure 6.3 – HD Weekly & Daily Charts (Source: Investing.com)
https://invst.ly/i67p0

The Money Management calculation determined that with an account size of $10,000 and an Account Risk of 1%, the maximum number of shares that can be safely bought will be 14 (see Table 6.1 and Figure 6.3). If the trade goes against the desired direction, and the Stop Loss is hit, the maximum loss will be $95.90 (=14*$6.85). In that case, the account size will reduce to $9,904.10 ($10,000 - $95.90), as shown in the example.

If, on the other hand, the stock price moves up and hits the profit target, the profit will be $191.80 (=14*$13.70). In that case, the account size will increase to $10,191.80.

Cash Account - Money Management Calculator	
Description	HD
Capital (Account Size)	$10,000
% Risk on Capital (Account Size)	1%
Account Risk	$100.00
Entry Price/Share	$217.09
Stop Loss Price/Share	$210.24
Trade Risk/Share	$6.85
Commission (assumed zero)	$0.00
Maximum Shares that can be bought	46
Risk Adjusted Maximum Trade Size	14
Optimal Position Size	14
Actual Account Risk	$95.90
Total Cost of the Trade	$3,039.26

Table 6.1 – HD Money Management Calculator

In the evening of Aug 20, 2019 or before market open of the next trading day (Aug 21, 2019), place 3 Orders:

"Buy Stop Limit Order" for 14 shares of HD with the Limit Price of $217.09, Stop Loss Price of $210.24 and Profit Target of $230.79. If the trading platform does not allow placing 3 Orders simultaneously, place the Buy Order first. Once the Buy Order is filled, place the remaining 2 Orders (Stop Loss and Profit Target). The Buy Order is a Day Order, and the other two are Good-Till-Cancel (GTC) Orders.

The Order will only be filled; if on Aug 21, 2019, the stock price touches the $217.09 mark. On Aug 21, 2019, the Buy Order was filled as the stock price touched the Limit Price of $217.09. Two other situations could have happened on Aug 21, 2019.

If on Aug 21, 2019, the range of the stock price was below the Limit Price of $217.09, the Buy Order would not have been filled. The Order would be void at the end of the trading day. This is good, because it is better to buy stocks which are continuing to move higher, and not lower.

On the other hand, if on Aug 21, 2019, the range of the stock price was above the Limit Price of $217.09, the Buy Order would not have been filled. The Order would be void at the end of the trading day. The stock price was too extended above the desired Limit Price. The Profit Target was hit on Sep 6, 2019, and the shares were sold for $230.79/share.

Risk = 14*$6.85 = $95.90
Total Profit = 14*($230.79 - $217.09)= $191.80
Reward to Risk Ratio = 191.80/95.90 = 2 : 1

Table 6.2 – HD Reward to Risk Ratio

On the other hand, if the Stop Loss price was touched before the Profit Target, 14 shares would have been sold for $210.24/share, with a total loss of $95.90 (= 14*$6.85). For simplicity, I had not included the commissions in the calculations.

EXAMPLE 2: WALMART (WMT)

As explained earlier, the Setup will occur when the Positive Directional Indicator (+DI) crosses above 25 on the daily chart. On Aug 15, 2019, all three conditions were met for this trade.

Condition 1: On the weekly chart of SPX, the price chart was smooth and trending up, 50 SMA was above 200 SMA, and the SPX price was above 50 SMA (same as HD example, see Figure 6.2).

Condition 2: On the weekly chart of Walmart (WMT), the price chart was smooth and trending up, 50 SMA was above 200 SMA, and +DI was above –DI (Figure 6.4).

Condition 3: On Aug 15, 2019, +DI crossed above 25 on the daily chart. The stock price was also above 50 SMA (Figure 6.4). The earnings were reported before the market open on Aug 15, 2019, so the next earnings will be reported about three months later.

The closing price of the stock on Aug 15, 2019, was $112.69, and ATR was 2.3527, say 2.35. Hence, the Trade Risk/share (Stop Loss) = 1.5*ATR = 1.5*$2.35 = $3.525, say $3.50. Stop Loss Price will be set at $109.19 (= $112.69 – $3.50). Profit Target = Buy Price + 2*Stop Loss = $119.69 (= $112.69 + 2*$3.5).

The Money Management calculation determined that with an account size of $10,000 and an Account Risk of 1%, the maximum number of shares that can be safely bought will be 28 (see Table 6.3 and Figure 6.4). If the trade goes against the desired direction, and the stop loss is hit, the maximum loss is $98.00 (=28*$3.5). In that case, the account size will reduce to $9,902.00 ($10,000 – $98.00), as shown in the example (Figure 6.4).

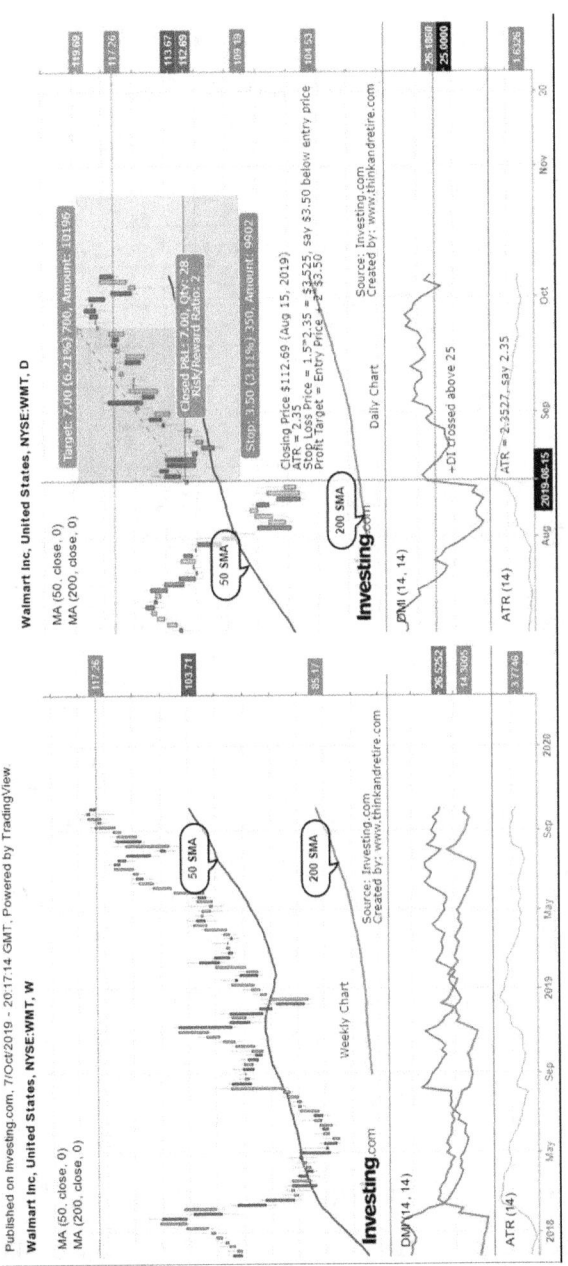

Figure 6.4 – WMT Weekly & Daily Charts (Source: Investing.com)
https://invst.ly/i67ck

If, on the other hand, the stock price moves up and hits the Profit Target, the profit will be $196.00 (= 28*$7.00). In that case, the account size will increase to $10,196.00, as shown in Figure 6.4.

Cash Account - Money Management Calculator	
Description	WMT
Capital (Account Size)	$10,000
% Risk on Capital (Account Size)	1%
Account Risk	$100.00
Entry Price/Share	$112.69
Stop Loss Price/Share	$109.19
Trade Risk/Share	$3.50
Commission (assumed zero)	$0.00
Maximum Shares that can be bought	88
Risk Adjusted Maximum Trade Size	28
Optimal Position Size	28
Actual Account Risk	$98.00
Total Cost of the Trade	$3,155.32

Table 6.3 – WMT Money Management Calculator

After the market closed on Aug 15, 2019 or before market open the next trading day (Aug 16, 2019), place 3 Orders: "Buy Stop Limit Order" for 28 shares of WMT with the Limit Price of $112.69, Stop Loss Price of $109.19 and Profit Target of $119.69.

On Aug 16, 2019, the Buy Order was filled as the stock price touched the Limit Price of $112.69. The Profit Target was reached on Sep 24, 2019, and the shares were sold for $119.69/share.

Risk = 28*$3.50 = $98.00
Total Profit = 28*($119.69 - $112.69) = $196.00
Reward to Risk Ratio = 196/98 = 2 : 1

Table 6.4 – WMT Reward to Risk Ratio

TRADING PLAN – MEDIUM TERM TREND TRADING

For medium-term trend trading, I will place the Initial Stop Loss at 3*ATR below the Buy Price. The term "Initial" is used as the Stop Loss Price will be raised as soon as the stock price rises and reaches a pre-determined price. This will be done to lock-in some profits.

ENTRY SETUP CRITERIA

A couple of my favorite Setups for medium-term trend trading are presented in this section. The Setup will occur when price breaks out through the top of the Bull Flag Pattern or Ascending Triangle Pattern, BOTH on the weekly and the daily charts of the stock, if other conditions are also satisfied. Many websites explaining different patterns are listed in Appendix B.

The shares will only be purchased when the following three conditions are met:

Condition 1: On the weekly price chart of the S&P 500 Index (SPX) (for US, use similar indices for other markets):

- Weekly price chart is smooth and trending up, and
- 50 SMA is above 200 SMA

Condition 2: On the weekly stock chart:

- Look at weekly price action for the past 8 to 10 years
- Weekly price chart is smooth and trending up
- 50 SMA is above 200 SMA, and
- Price breaks out through the top of the Bull Flag Pattern or some other consolidation patterns with a higher volume

Condition 3: On the daily stock chart:

- Price is above 50 SMA or just crossed above 50 SMA
- No earnings announcements within the next 3 to 4 weeks, and
- Price breaks out through the top of the Bull Flag Pattern or some other consolidation patterns with a higher volume

The question may arise as how to find the stocks which are breaking out of these patterns. It can be done visually on the stock charts. Some websites offer the pattern breakouts info, such as Chartmill.com for US stocks.

- https://www.chartmill.com/trading-ideas/13-Bull-Flags?affl=84995

Once a list of stocks is obtained, do a quick check if these stocks meet the following mandatory criteria:

- **Average Volume:** need liquidity, so pick stocks which trade more than 500K/day on average (of 30 days), thereby avoiding stocks which trade at low volumes,
- **Exchange:** interested in stocks trading at reputed exchanges,
- **Index:** interested in S&P 500 Index stocks (for US, use similar indices for other markets),
- **Last (Price):** need the stock price to be over $10. Not interested in low-priced or penny stocks,
- **Market Capitalization:** interested in stocks which are midcap (+2B) and higher [including (large-cap (+10B) and mega-cap (+200B)],
- **Sector:** focus on the Leading Sectors, and
- **Simple Moving Average (SMA 50) above 200 SMA (on a daily chart):** want the 50 SMA to be above 200 SMA to ensure that we are in an uptrend.

TRIGGER PRICE

As soon as the stock price is breaking out through the top of the Bull Flag Pattern or some other consolidation patterns on the weekly chart, open the daily stock chart. Identify on which day on the daily chart, the price is breaking out through the top of the patterns (say, that is Day 1). Note the closing price and the ATR value.

Then use the "Long Position" tool of TradingView.com or Investing.com or the Money Management calculator to determine the Maximum Position size (maximum number of shares to buy safely). After the market is closed on Day 1 or before the market opens on Day 2, a Market Buy Order will be placed to enter the long position. As soon as the market opens on Day 2, the Order will be filled. Note the Buy Price.

STOP LOSS PRICE

For medium-term trend trading, my Initial Stop Loss is 3*ATR. Therefore, the Initial Stop Loss Price = "Buy Price – 3*ATR".

After the stock price has risen to a certain level, increase the Stop Loss Price to just above the Buy Price, I usually use "Buy Price + $0.25". In Example 1, the Stop Loss was raised after the stock price reached Profit Target 1. In Example 2, the Stop Loss was raised after the stock price has risen by the Initial Stop Loss (risk) amount (i.e., 3*ATR).

PROFIT TARGET

For medium-term trend trading, I will sell the shares in two stages. The Profit Targets will vary depending on the Setups chosen, as illustrated in the examples to follow. Sell half the shares when Profit Target 1 is reached. There are many ways to manage the trade. The traders can decide where to take profits. This book is just illustrating a few examples.

For the remaining half of the shares, use trailing stops, or just sit tight (i.e., do not change the Stop Loss any further) and wait until certain other technical conditions are met (say 20 SMA crosses below 50 SMA, or 50 SMA crosses below 200 SMA, and so on).

To avoid micro-managing the trade, leave the Stop Loss Price at "Buy Price + $0.25" and wait for the stock price to rise until 50 SMA crosses below 200 SMA on the daily chart (as illustrated in the examples).

MEDIUM TERM TREND TRADING EXAMPLES

EXAMPLE 1: ESTEE LAUDER (EL)

The stock price breaking out above the "Bull Flag Pattern" with higher volume is selected as the entry criteria for this example. Details about "Bull Flag Pattern" are provided in the "Chart Patterns" links of Appendix B.

On May 03, 2017, all the following three conditions were met:

Condition 1: On the SPX weekly chart, the price pattern was smooth and trending up, and 50 SMA was above 200 SMA (same as HD example, see Figure 6.2).

Condition 2: On the weekly chart of Estee Lauder (EL), the price pattern was smooth and trending up, 50 SMA was above 200 SMA, and the stock price broke out through the top of the Bull Flag Pattern during the week of May 01, 2017 with a higher volume (Figure 6.5).

Condition 3: On May 03, 2017, stock price broke out through the top of the Bull Flag Pattern with a higher volume on the daily chart. The stock price was above 50 SMA (Figure 6.6). The earnings were reported before the market opened on May 03, 2017 (same morning), so there will be no earnings announcements in the next three months.

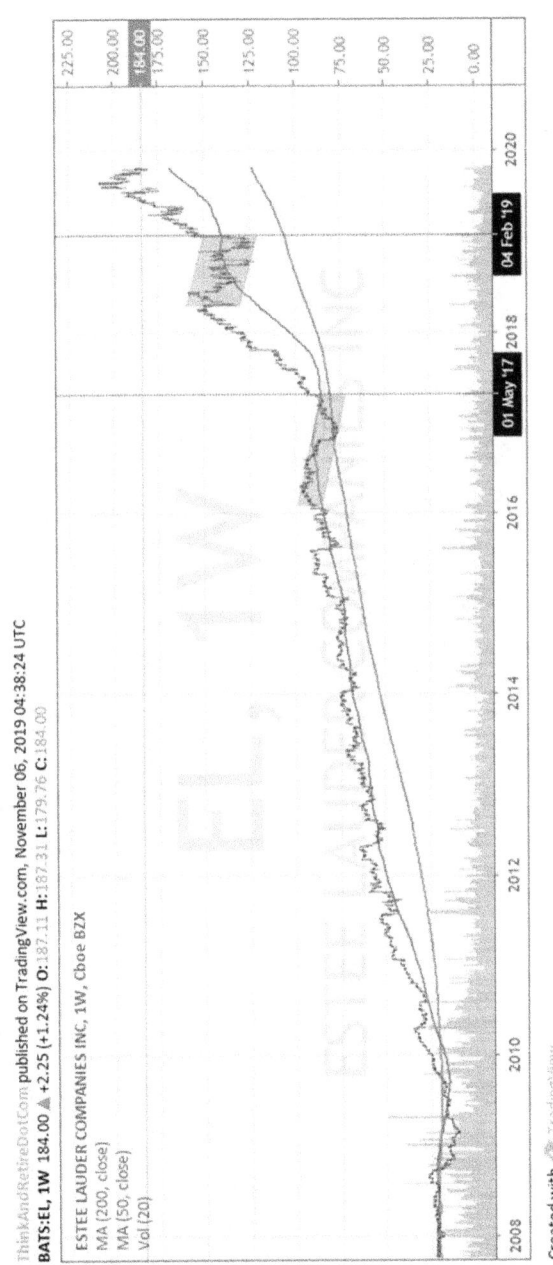

Figure 6.5 – EL Weekly Chart (Source: TradingView.com)
https://www.tradingview.com/x/wDnHSdXw/

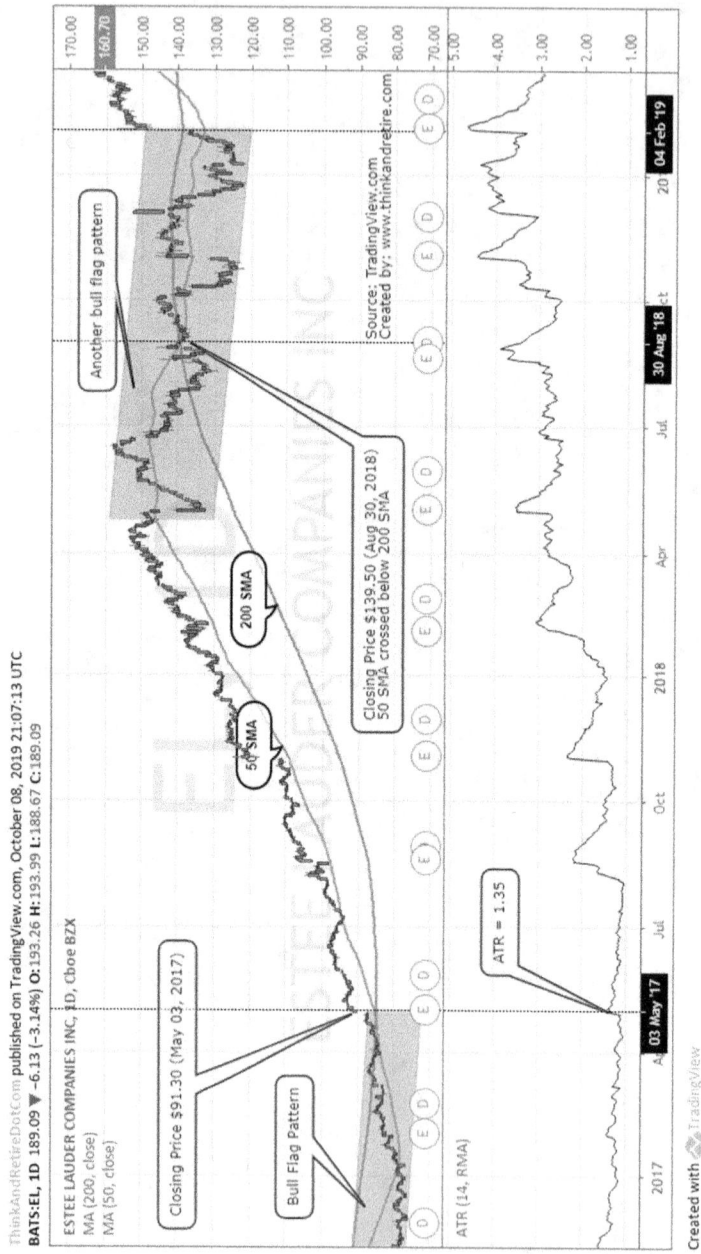

Figure 6.6 – EL Daily Chart (Source: TradingView.com)
https://www.tradingview.com/x/Oahp6lLK/

The closing stock price on May 03, 2017, was $91.30, and ATR was 1.35. The width of the flag was about $15.00. Therefore, Trade Risk/share (Stop Loss) = 3*ATR = 3*$1.35 = $4.05. Initial Stop Loss Price will be set at $87.25 (= Buy Price – 3*ATR = $91.30 – 3*$1.35).

In this example, the Stop Loss was raised to "Buy Price +$0.25" after the Profit Target 1 was reached. Profit Target 1 = Buy Price + Flag width = $91.30 + $15.00 = $106.30.

The Money Management calculation determined that with an account size of $10,000 and Account Risk of 1%, the maximum number of shares that can be safely bought was 24 (see Table 6.5).

The above information was used for planning purposes before buying the shares. The actual buy price will be different, as it will depend on the stock's opening price the next day.

Cash Account - Money Management Calculator	
Description	EL
Capital (Account Size)	$10,000
% Risk on Capital (Account Size)	1%
Account Risk	$100.00
Entry Price/Share	$91.30
Stop Loss Price/Share	$87.25
Trade Risk/Share	$4.05
Commission (assumed zero)	$0.00
Maximum Shares that can be bought	109
Risk Adjusted Maximum Trade Size	24
Optimal Position Size	24
Actual Account Risk	$97.20
Total Cost of the Trade	$2,191.20

Table 6.5 – EL Money Management Calculator

After the market closes on May 03, 2017 or before market opens next trading day (May 04, 2017), simultaneously place 3 Orders (if the trading platform allows that): Buy 24 shares of EL at Market Price, Initial Stop Loss Price of $87.25 (for 24 shares, Good till Cancel Order) and Sell 12 shares at Limit Price of $106.30 (Profit Target 1, Good Till Cancel Order). If the broker does not allow to place these 3 Orders simultaneously, first place the Buy Order. After the Buy Order is filled, place the Stop Loss and Profit Target Orders.

On May 04, 2017, the stock opening price was $91.46, so the actual Risk = $4.21 (= $91.46 - $87.25).

On Aug 18, 2017, the stock price touched Profit Target 1 ($106.30), and 12 shares were sold. On the same day or next day, increase the Stop Loss from $87.25 to $91.71 (= Buy price $91.46 + $0.25). Now, we have locked in some profits, and the trade cannot lose money on the remaining shares (no guarantees on the stock market!).

Conservative traders can increase the Stop Loss price from $87.25 to $91.71 after the stock price has increased by the initial Stop Loss value. In this example that would be when the stock price reached $95.51 (= Buy Price + 3*ATR = $91.46 + 3*$1.35). It happened on Jun 02, 2017 (i.e., lot earlier than Aug 18, 2017).

Let the price rise until the 50 SMA crosses below 200 SMA on the daily chart. It happened on Aug 30, 2018. On that day, the closing price was $139.50. On the evening of Aug 30, 2018, place a Sell Order for the remaining 12 shares at the market price for the next trading day (Aug 31, 2018). The market opened at $139.34 on Aug 31, 2018, and that will likely be the Sell price for the remaining 12 shares. (I said "likely", because sometimes slippages occur due to gaps or other overnight news events).

Risk = 24*($91.46-$87.25)= $101.04
Profit 1 = 12*$106.30-$91.46) = $178.08
Profit 2 = 12*($139.34 - $91.46) =$574.56
Total Profit = $752.64 (=$178.08 + $574.56)
Reward to Risk Ratio = 752.64/101.04 = 7.45 : 1

Table 6.6 – EL Reward to Risk Ratio

Since the stock opened a bit higher ($91.46 vs. $91.30) on May 04, 2017, the risk ($101.04) was slightly higher. As this was a nominal amount, I kept the risk as is. If the stock had opened a lot higher than the previous day's close, I would have increased the Stop Limit Price accordingly to keep the Account risk within $100.

EXAMPLE 2: MCCORMICK & COMPANY (MKC)

The stock price breaking out above the "Ascending Triangle Pattern" with higher volume is selected as the entry criteria in this example. Details about the "Ascending Triangle Pattern" is provided in the "Chart Patterns" hyperlinks of Appendix B. On Jun 28, 2018, all the following three conditions were met.

Condition 1: On the SPX weekly chart, the price pattern was smooth and trending up, and 50 SMA was above 200 SMA (same as HD example, see Figure 6.2).

Condition 2: On the weekly chart of McCormick & Company (MKC), the price pattern was smooth and trending up. 50 SMA was above 200 SMA. The stock price broke out through the top of the Ascending Triangle Pattern during the week of Jun 25, 2018, with a higher volume (see Figure 6.7).

Condition 3: On Jun 28, 2018, stock price broke out through the top of the Ascending Triangle Pattern with a higher volume on the daily chart. The stock price was above 50 SMA (see Figure 6.8). The earnings were reported before the market opened on Jun 28, 2018 (same morning), so no earnings are expected in the next three months.

The closing stock price on Jun 28, 2018, was $114.83, and ATR was 2.54. The thickest point of the Ascending Triangle was about $20. Initial Stop Loss Price = Buy Price − 3*ATR = $114.83 − 3*$2.54 = $107.21.

In this example, the Stop Loss will be raised to "Buy Price + $0.25" after the stock price rises by the amount of Initial Risk of 3*ATR. Profit Target 1 = Buy Price + Thickest point of the Ascending Triangle = $114.83 + $20.00 = $134.83.

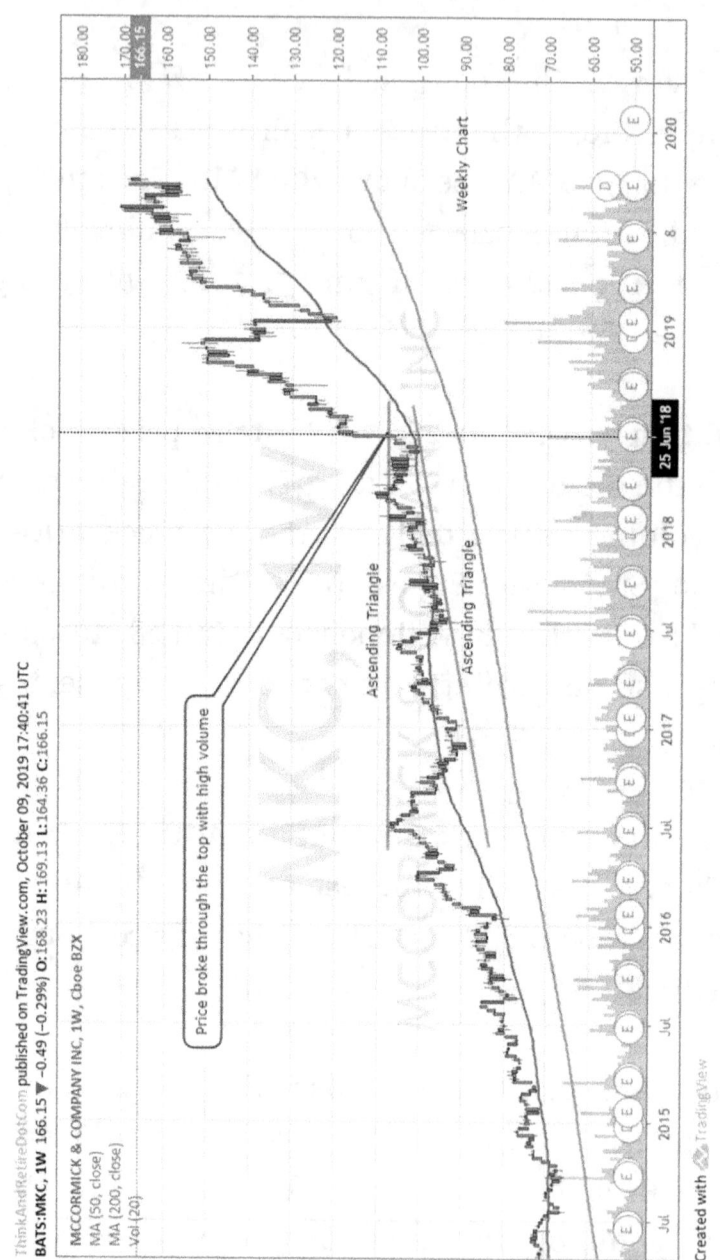

Figure 6.7 – MKC Weekly Chart (Source: TradingView.com)
https://www.tradingview.com/x/QQEsBSMC/

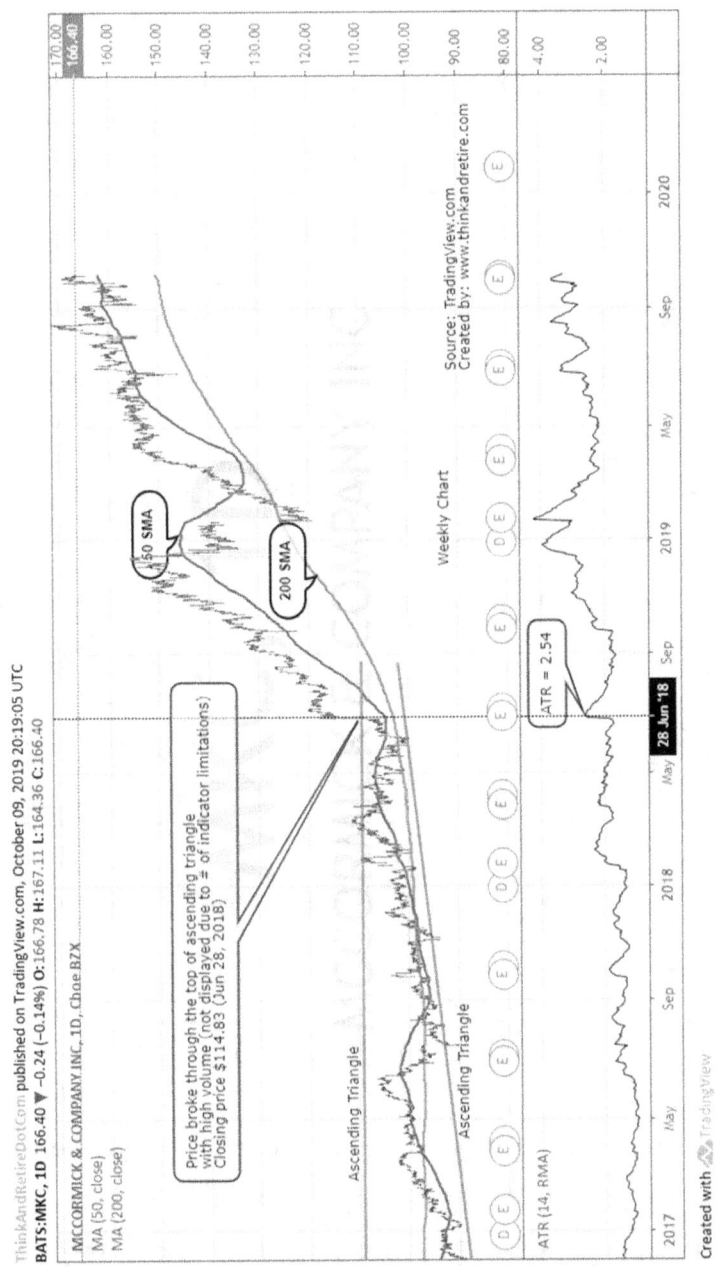

Figure 6.8 – MKC Daily Chart (Source: TradingView.com)
https://www.tradingview.com/x/2WY3R4Wq/

The Money Management calculation determined that with an account size of $10,000 and Account Risk of 1%, the maximum number of shares that can be safely bought was 13 (see Table 6.7).

The above information was used for planning before buying the shares. The actual stock buy price will be different; it will depend on the stock opening price the next day.

Cash Account - Money Management Calculator	
Description	MKC
Capital (Account Size)	$10,000
% Risk on Capital (Account Size)	1%
Account Risk	$100.00
Entry Price/Share	$114.83
Stop Loss Price/Share	$107.21
Trade Risk/Share	$7.62
Commission (assumed zero)	$0.00
Maximum Shares that can be bought	87
Risk Adjusted Maximum Trade Size	13
Optimal Position Size	13
Actual Account Risk	$99.06
Total Cost of the Trade	$1,492.79

Table 6.7 – MKC Money Management Calculator

After the market closes on Jun 28, 2018 or before market opens next trading day (Jun 29, 2018), simultaneously place 3 Orders (if the trading platform allows that): Buy 13 shares of MKC at Market Price, Initial

Stop Loss Price of $107.21 (for 13 shares, Good till Cancel Order) and Sell 6 shares at Limit Price of $134.83 (Profit Target 1, Good Till Cancel Order). If the broker does not allow to place these 3 Orders simultaneously, first place the Buy Order. After the Buy Order is filled, place the Stop Loss and Profit Target Orders.

On Jun 29, 2018, MKC opened at $115.09, so that will be the Buy price. To keep the Account Risk below $100, the Stop Loss Price needs to be increased to $107.47 (= $115.09 - 3*2.54). Profit Target 1 need to be increased to $135.09 (= $115.09 + $20.00).

An alert was set in TradingView.com or Investing.com to inform as soon as the MKC price reaches $122.71 (= $115.09 + 3*ATR = $115.09 + 3*$2.54), i.e. the stock price rises by the initial risk amount, so that I can raise the Stop Loss to protect my profits. On Aug 15, 2018, TradingView.com alerted that the stock price has reached $122.71, so the Stop Loss Price was increased to $115.34 (= Buy Price + $0.25 = $115.09 + $0.25) on that day.

On Oct 2, 2018, the stock price touched Profit Target 1 ($135.09), and six shares were sold.

Let the price rise. The remaining seven shares will be sold when 50 SMA crosses below 200 SMA on the daily chart. At the time of writing this book, the 50 SMA is still above 200 SMA. At this stage, there are a few options:

- Let the price take its course of action until 50 SMA crosses below 200 SMA, or
- Sell the remaining seven shares now and lock in the profits, or
- Use Trailing Stop Loss and ride the upward movement of the stock price until the Trailing Stop Loss is hit. There are many ways to set the Trailing Stop (fixed $, fixed %, Chandelier Exit, price structure such as swing lows, dynamic stop loss such as moving averages, and so on).

At the time of writing, in this trade, we have the following data.

Risk = 13*3*$2.54 = $99.06
Profit 1 = 6*$20.00 = $120.00
Profit 2 = 7*($.......... - $115.09) = $...............
Total Profit = $........... (=$120.00 + $...............)
Reward to Risk Ratio = .../99.06 = ... : 1

Table 6.8 – MKC Reward to Risk Ratio

TRADING PLAN – LONG TERM TREND TRADING

I will present a different concept for long term trading. Moving Averages and Relative Strength of the stock (compared to the broader stock market) will be used to guide the entries and the exits. The "Relative Strength" was briefly discussed in Chapter 4. We will use the second method of calculating Relative Strength in this Chapter. In this method, Relative Strength is calculated by dividing the stock price by the Index price and plotting the result.

As this is a long-term strategy, ensure that the company is an established business and has been around for a long time before considering buying their shares.

ENTRY SETUP CRITERIA

The main entry criteria for buying a stock in this strategy is when both the Stock Price and the Relative Strength line are both rising (sloping up) at the same time (see right side of Figure 6.9). Even if the stock price is in an uptrend, but the Relative Strength line is flat or sloping down, there will be no new entry.

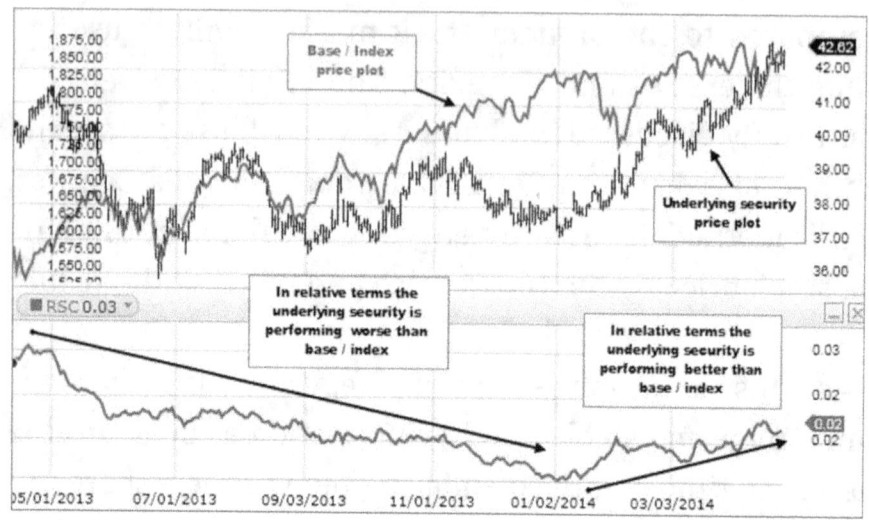

Figure 6.9 – Relative Strength Line (Source: Fidelity.com)

The left side of the chart shows that the Relative Strength line is sloping down, although the stock price is relatively flat. Therefore, no new entry for that stock.

I will add one more rule to ensure that the stock price is in an uptrend. I want to ensure that 50 SMA is above or just crossed above 200 SMA on the daily chart.

As this is a long-term approach, we need to plot a daily chart spanning about 5 to 10 years. Add 50 SMA, 200 SMA, and Relative Strength Line (SPX) indicators on the daily chart.

Few things to note about the "Relative Strength Line (SPX)" indicator:

- I have used the one available in TradingView.com (in charts) under Indicators & Strategies -> Public Library > Relative Strength Line (by "victoryong"),
- Need to change the Index from SPX to the appropriate Index of your market.

Now the question is how to find these stocks. There are two ways to do it:

- Click each of the stocks in the Watchlist (Chapter 3) and view the corresponding charts in TradingView.com (chart settings shown in the examples to follow), or
- By scanning for stocks (in Leading Sectors), which have 50 SMA above 200 SMA.

There will be some requirements for visual interpretation of charts in this strategy. A good understanding of Trend lines and Consolidation Patterns would be helpful.

Two examples are discussed for long term trading. Example 1 discusses one of the Leading Stocks (SRE, Sempra Energy) in the Utilities Sector. For Example 2, use the "Stock Screener" feature of TradingView.com and scan for top stocks in the Non-Cyclicals Sector (a Leading Sector) (https://www.tradingview.com/screener/). Use eight additional filters for the selection process, as indicated below.

- **Symbol type:** only interested in common stocks,
- **Average Volume:** need liquidity, so picked stocks which trade more than 500K/day on average (of 30 days), thereby avoiding stocks which trade at low volumes,
- **Exchange:** interested in stocks trading at reputed exchanges,
- **Index:** interested in S&P 500 Index stocks (for US, use similar indices for other markets),
- **Last (Price):** need the stock price to be over $10. Not interested in low-priced or penny stocks,
- **Market Capitalization:** interested in stocks which are midcap (+2B) and higher [including (large-cap (+10B) and mega-cap (+200B)],
- **Sector:** focussed on Non-Cyclicals Sector (for Example 2), and
- **Simple Moving Average (SMA 50) above 200 SMA:** want the 50 SMA to be above 200 SMA to ensure that we are in an uptrend.

The search indicated that 22 stocks met the criteria. They are sorted by weekly performance (as of market close Oct 13, 2019). The top weekly performer was TSN (Tyson Foods). We will examine this stock in Example 2.

Go through the list of these stocks and plot them on a daily chart with three technical indicators: 50 SMA, 200 SMA, and Relative Strength Line (SPX). Study the charts and see if both the Relative Strength Line and the stock price are rising (sloping up), and the 50 SMA is above 200 SMA on the daily chart.

TRIGGER PRICE

As soon as the Entry Setup criteria are met on a daily chart, wait for the price to retrace back to some support level (such as 50 SMA or 200 SMA). Then place a Buy Limit Order or a Market Order.

Note the approximate stock price and the ATR value to calculate the possible Buy price and Risk per share (i.e., Stop Loss, which will be about 6 to 8*ATR for the long-term trend trading strategy). The Money Management Calculator will then determine the maximum number of shares to buy based on the risk tolerance levels.

One thing to note is that the free version of TradingView.com restricts the number of indicators to 3, so we need to find ATR value from another charting source (such as Investing.com). Once the Buy Order is filled, we will note the Buy Price and the ATR value of that day.

STOP LOSS PRICE

For long-term trend trading, my Stop Loss is 6 to 8*ATR. Generally, for the Technology Sector, I use 8*ATR as the Stop Loss, to give more room for their usual price fluctuations.

PROFIT TARGET

For long-term trend trading, I am usually more flexible with the Profit Targets. A few options are presented below. Traders can be creative based on their personal choices.

Option 1: As soon as the price moves up by 3*ATR (half of the Initial Stop Loss amount), raise the Stop Loss to "Buy Price + $0.25". This will protect the trade from any potential loss. Sell all positions when 50 SMA crosses below 200 SMA, as shown in the examples below. This option has a higher profit potential and less commission costs. However, the risk is that the price can briefly touch the new Stop Loss price and the shares are sold and you are out of the trade.

Option 2: As soon as the price moves up by 3*ATR (half of the Initial Stop Loss amount), raise the Stop Loss to "Buy Price + $0.25". Scale the exits. It will depend on the number of shares. If 1000 shares are purchased, maybe sell 100 (or its multiples) shares every time the stock price rises by a certain amount (fixed $, fixed %, x*ATR, and so on). Sell the last portion of the shares when the 50 SMA crosses below 200 SMA. This option will lock in profits at every rise in stock prices. However, the commission costs will be higher as there will be more trades.

Option 3: Same as Option 2, with the exception that continuously raise the Stop Loss (called Trailing Stop Loss) (by fixed $, fixed %, fixed ATR, etc.) until the Stop Loss is hit. This option will have the benefits of locking in higher profits, and a chance of being stopped out at a higher price. The commission costs will be higher.

Option 4: As soon as the price moves up by 6*ATR (Initial Stop Loss amount), raise the Stop Loss to "Buy Price + 3*ATR". Sell all positions when 50 SMA crosses below 200 SMA or when both the Relative Strength Line and the stock price have stopped rising simultaneously.

There are no right or wrong options for exiting a position. The traders must choose which option works best for them.

LONG TERM TREND TRADING EXAMPLES

Two trade examples are presented for this strategy – stock symbols SRE and TSN. SRE (Sempra Energy) was one of the Leading Stocks from the Utilities Sector (one of the Leading Sectors, Chapter 4). TSN (Tyson Foods) came up as the top weekly performer (discussed earlier in this Chapter) from the Consumer Non-Cyclicals Sector (one of the Leading Sectors, Chapter 4).

Entry Setup Criteria, as discussed earlier, are summarized below. On the daily chart of the stock:
- Relative Strength Line is sloping up,
- Stock price is rising, and
- 50 SMA is above or just crossed above the 200 SMA

EXAMPLE 1: SEMPRA ENERGY (SRE)

The daily chart of SRE from 2009 to 2019 is presented (divided into 2 charts).

CHART 1

We will study the Chart 1 (Figure 6.10) for the period from 2009 to end of 2014.

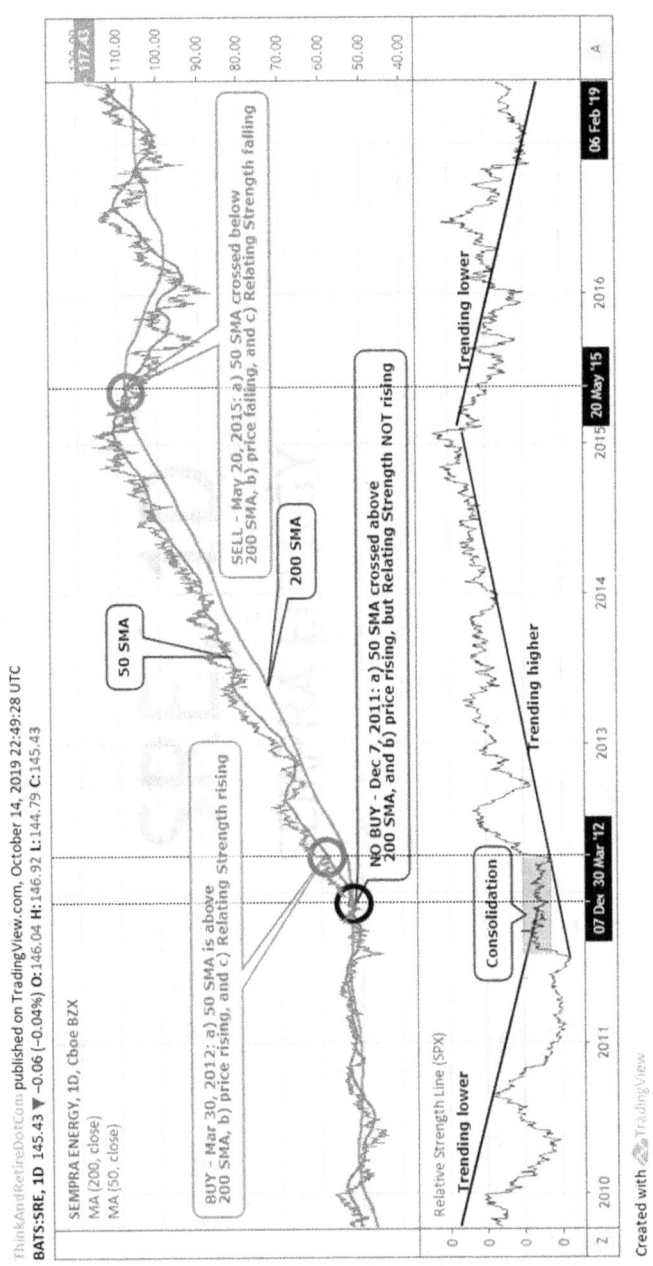

Figure 6.10 – SRE Daily Chart 1 (Source: TradingView.com)
https://www.tradingview.com/x/OEYolq9h/

The observations from Chart 1 (Figure 6.10) are summarized in Table 6.9.

Chart 1: SRE Daily Chart		
Time window	Relative Strength Line	Price Action
2009 to late 2011	Sloping down	Flat
Late 2011 to early 2012	Flat (consolidation)	Flat
Early 2012 to end of 2014	Sloping up	Rising
Buy Setup on Mar 30, 2012, Closing price = $59.96, ATR(14) = $0.8418 (source: Investing.com). Sell on May 20, 2015, Closing Price = $107.75. Risk = 6*$0.8418 = $5.05/share. Profit = $107.75 - $59.96 = $47.79/share. Reward to Risk ratio = 9.5 : 1 (Exit Option 1).		

Table 6.9 – SRE Daily Chart 1 Observations

The Buy Setup occurred on Mar 30, 2012 (shown by a green circle on Figure 6.10 and discussed in Table 6.9). The Buy Price will be $59.96. ATR was $0.8418; therefore, the Risk was $5.05/share (6*ATR). The Sell Price was $107.75 on May 20, 2015. The Reward to Risk Ratio was 9.5 : 1.

A detailed price action around the buy date of Mar 30, 2012 is shown in Figure 6.11. It shows that the price difference between the Closing Price and Support 1 was $2.23 (= $59.96 - $57.73). The price difference between the Closing Price and Support 2 was $2.93 (=$59.96 - $57.03).

Both these values ($2.23 and $2.93) were significantly smaller than the Risk/share of $5.05 (= 6*ATR), so our choice of 6*ATR as Stop Loss gave the stock price more breathing room (for price fluctuation) than what was needed.

If we had reduced the Stop Loss to 3*ATR or 4*ATR, our risk of being stopped out would have been higher, but our Reward to Risk Ratio would have improved.

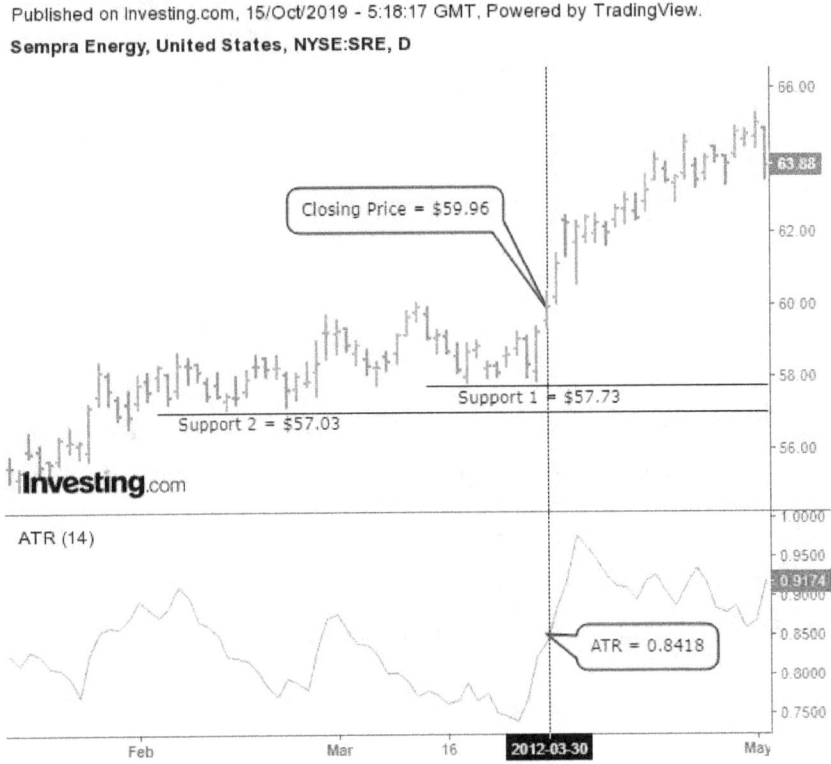

Figure 6.11 – Price action around Mar 30, 2012
(Source: Investing.com) - https://invst.ly/ke62c

CHART 2

We will study Chart 2 (Figure 6.12) for the period from early 2015 to the end of 2019. The observations from Chart 2 are in Table 6.10.

Chart 2: SRE Daily Chart		
Time window	Relative Strength Line	Price Action
Early 2015 to end of 2017	Sloping down	Flat
Early 2018 to end of 2018	Flat (consolidation)	Flat
End of 2018 to end of 2019	Sloping up	Rising
Buy Setup on Feb 6, 2019, Closing price = $117.75, ATR(14) = $1.8741 (source: Investing.com). As of Oct 14, 2019, the position was still Open (with Exit Option 1). Risk = 6*$1.8741 = $11.25/share.		

Table 6.10 – SRE Daily Chart 2 Observations

The Buy Setup occurred on Feb 06, 2019 (shown by a green circle in Figure 6.12 and discussed in Table 6.10). The Buy Price will be $117.75. ATR was $1.8741; therefore, the Risk was $11.25/share (6*ATR). The position was still open at the time of writing this Chapter.

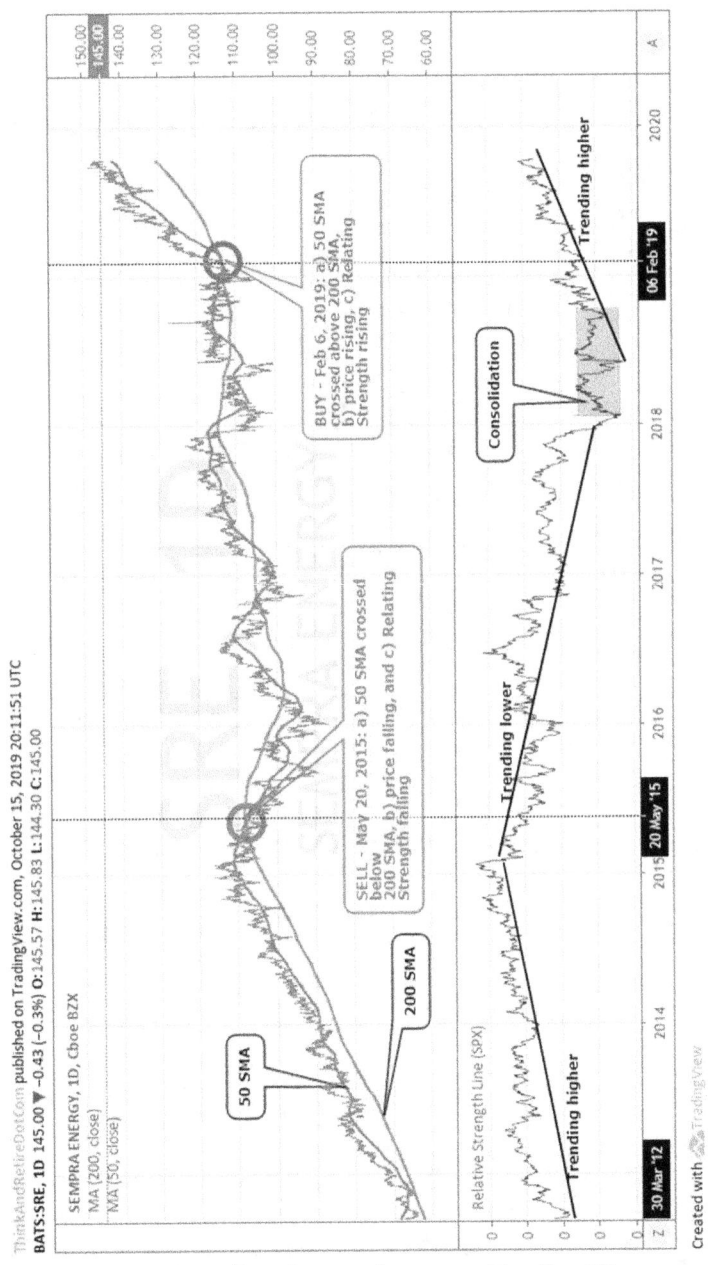

Figure 6.12 – SRE Daily Chart 2 (Source: TradingView.com)
https://www.tradingview.com/x/u1PfdjUK/

EXAMPLE 2: TYSON FOODS (TSN)

The daily price chart of TSN from the end of 2012 to end of 2019 is shown in Figure 6.13. The observations from the TSN chart are in Table 6.11. Note the 3 Buy Setups and the corresponding Reward to Risk Ratios in Table 6.12.

Chart: TSN Daily Chart		
Time window	**Relative Strength Line**	**Price Action**
End of 2012 to mid 2014	Sloping up	Rising
Mid 2014 to mid 2015	Flat (consolidation)	Flat
Mid 2015 to end of 2016	Sloping up	Rising
End of 2016 to mid 2018	Sloping down	Choppy (up and down)
Mid 2018 to end of 2018	Flat (consolidation)	Falling
Early 2019 to end of 2019	Sloping up	Rising
Note: 3 Buy Setups were identified as noted with 3 green circles on the chart		

Table 6.11 – TSN Daily Chart Observations

Buy Setups of TSN		
Setup No.	**Details**	**Reward to Risk Ratio**
1	14 Dec 2012 – Buy @ close: $19.65, ATR(14) =$0.3445, Risk = 6*$0.3445 = $2.07/share 23 Jul 2014 – Sell @ close: $39.29, Profit per share = $19.64 ($39.29 - $19.65)	**9.5 : 1**
2	10 Aug 2015 – Buy @ close: $42.85, ATR(14) =$1.0571, Risk = 6*$1.0571 = $6.34/share 25 Oct 2016 – Sell @ close: $69.04, Profit per share = $26.19 ($69.04 - $42.85)	**4.1 : 1**
3	22 Mar 2019 – Buy @ close: $66.61, ATR(14) =$1.2582, Risk = 6*$1.2582 = $7.55/share As of Oct 15, 2019, the Position was still open	**Open Position**
Note: ATR values obtained from Investing.com		

Table 6.12 – Buy Setups of TSN

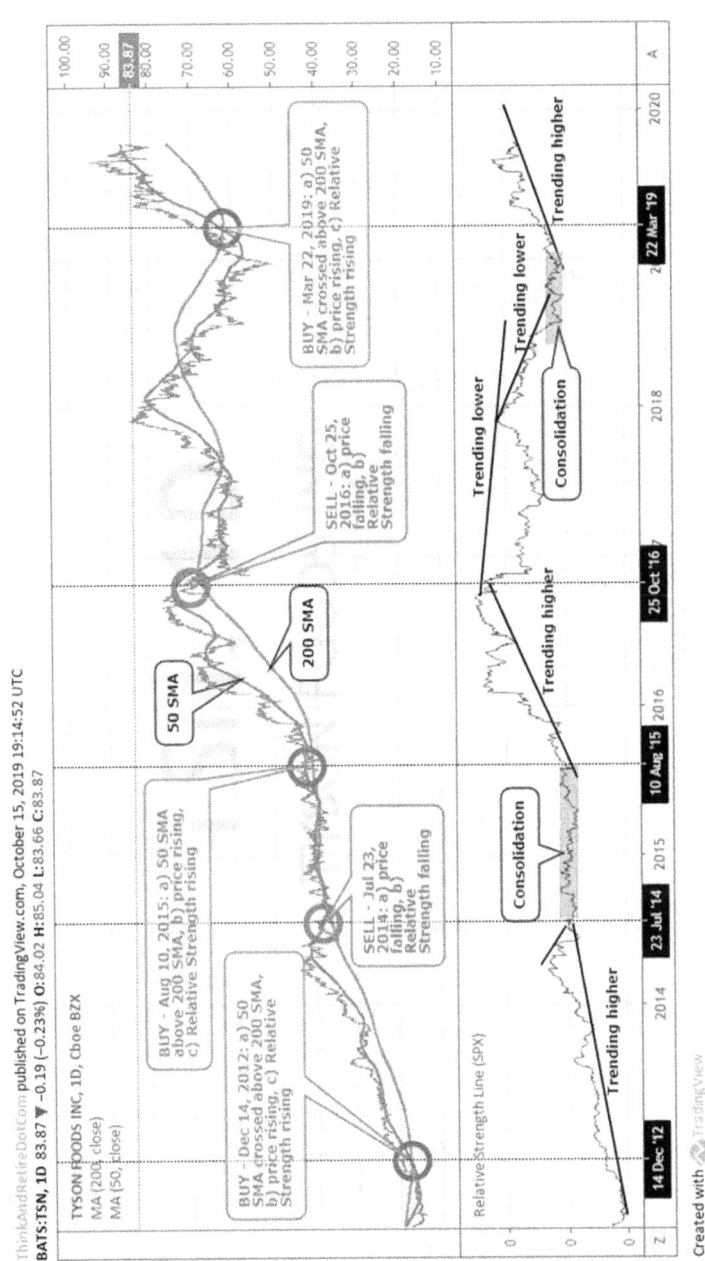

Figure 6.13 – TSN Daily Chart (Source: TradingView.com)
https://www.tradingview.com/x/A39TLS9Y/

SUMMARY

Table 6.13 below summarizes the Entry Setup Criteria, Trade Risk/share (Stop Loss), and Profit Targets as discussed in this Chapter.

	Short term	Medium term	Long term
Entry Setup criteria	**Weekly SPX chart** Trending up, 50 SMA > 200 SMA, SPX price > 50 SMA **Weekly stock chart** Trending up, 50 SMA > 200 SMA, + DI (14) > - DI(14) **Daily stock chart** +DI(14) crossed above 25, Stock price above 50 SMA or just crossed above 50 SMA, No earnings in next 3 to 4 weeks	**Weekly SPX chart** Trending up, 50 SMA > 200 SMA **Weekly stock chart** Trending up, 50 SMA > 200 SMA, Price breaks out above Bull Flag, Ascending Triangle or other consolidation patterns with a higher volume **Daily stock chart** Stock price above 50 SMA or just crossed above 50 SMA, No earnings in next 3 to 4 weeks, Stock price breaks out above Bull Flag, Ascending Triangle or other consolidation patterns with a higher volume	**Daily stock chart** Relative Strength line rising, Stock price rising, 50 SMA > 200 SMA
Trade Risk per share (Stop Loss)	1.5*ATR(14), Initial Stop Loss Price = Buy Price – 1.5*ATR, No Stop Loss adjustment	3*ATR(14), Initial Stop Loss Price = Buy price – 3*ATR, Example 1 – Stop Loss raised to "Buy Price + $0.25" after Profit Target 1 is reached, Example 2 – Stop Loss raised to "Buy Price + $0.25" after stock price had risen by 3*ATR	6*ATR, Initial Stop Loss Price = Buy Price – 6*ATR, Stop Loss raised to "Buy Price + $0.25" after stock price had risen by 3*ATR (half of Trade Risk)
Profit Target(s)	Buy Price + 3*ATR	Profit Target 1 – Variable, Profit Target 2 – Price at which 50 SMA crosses below 200 SMA on the daily chart	Profit Target = Sell when 50 SMA crosses below 200 SMA, or when Relative Strength line and stock price have stopped rising together

Table 6.13 – Summary Table of Example Trades

TIP

Trading is more of an art than a science.

Do not plan to catch every "Tops" and "Bottoms" of a stock price move.

The profits can be boosted with the help of Options.

If a good dividend paying stock is selected for the medium-term and long-term trend trading strategies, it will also generate a regular passive income stream.

If there is less time and desire for doing research, buying a low-cost index fund regularly, and holding it for the long-term by taking advantage of the Dollar Cost Average strategy (hyperlink below) is a good option.

- https://www.investopedia.com/terms/d/dollarco staveraging.asp

CHAPTER 7: TRADING JOURNAL

"Only the game can teach you the game." –
Jesse Livermore

A Trading Journal is a spreadsheet for performance management of trades. Trading Journal can be used for the following reasons:

- Track progress of trades
- Record Setups used for entries and exits
- Study winning trades
- Study losing trades
- Lessons learned, and many others.

A simple and easy to follow Trading Journal spreadsheet is shown in Table 7.1.

Buy Date	Stock Symbol	Strategy	# of shares	Buy Price per share ($)	Comm ($)	Total Cost ($)	Risk Per Share ($)	Total Risk ($)	Sell Date	Sell Price per share ($)	Comm ($)	Proceeds ($)	Profit/Loss ($)	Reward to Risk Ratio	Comments
Aug 21, 2019	HD	ST	14	$217.09	$0.00	$3,039.26	$6.85	$95.90	Sep 6, 2019	$230.79	$0.00	$3,231.06	$191.80	2.00	
Aug 16, 2019	WMT	ST	28	$112.69	$0.00	$3,155.32	$3.50	$98.00	Sep 24, 2019	$119.69	$0.00	$3,351.32	$196.00	2.00	
May 04, 2017	EL	MT	12	$91.46	$0.00	$1,097.52	$4.21	$50.52	Aug 18, 2017	$106.30	$0.00	$1,275.60	$178.08	3.52	half position
May 04 2017	EL	MT	12	$91.46	$0.00	$1,097.52	$4.21	$50.52	Aug 31, 2018	$139.34	$0.00	$1,672.08	$574.56	11.37	half position
Jun 29, 2018	MKC	MT	6	$115.09	$0.00	$690.54	$7.62	$45.72	Oct 2, 2018	$135.09	$0.00	$810.54	$120.00	2.62	partial position
Jun 29, 2018	MKC	MT	7	$115.09	$0.00	$805.63	$7.62	$53.34			$0.00	$0.00	-$805.63	-15.10	OPEN
Mar 30, 2012	SRE	LT	1	$59.96	$0.00	$59.96	$5.05	$5.05	May 20, 2015	$107.75	$0.00	$107.75	$47.79	9.46	
Feb 6, 2019	SRE	LT	1	$117.75	$0.00	$117.75	$11.25	$11.25			$0.00	$0.00	-$117.75		OPEN
Dec 14, 2012	TSN	LT	1	$19.65	$0.00	$19.65	$2.07	$2.07	Jul 23, 2014	$39.29	$0.00	$39.29	$19.64	9.49	
Aug 10, 2015	TSN	LT	1	$42.85	$0.00	$42.85	$6.34	$6.34	Oct 25, 2016	$69.04	$0.00	$69.04	$26.19	4.13	
Mar 22 2019	TSN	LT	1	$66.61	$0.00	$66.61	$7.55	$7.55			$0.00	$0.00	-$66.61	-8.82	OPEN

Note: Assumed zero commission for discussion. In actual trading, there will be commissions which needs to be factored into actual profit/loss calculation

For Short Term (ST) Trading, assumed Risk/share = 1.5*ATR

For Medium Term (MT) Trading, assumed Risk/share = 3*ATR

For Long Term (LT) Trading assumed Risk/share = 6*ATR

Table 7.1 – Trading Journal

An editable and downloadable version of the Trading Journal is included in the FREE Bonus (Appendix D).

The Trading Journal keeps track of profits and losses for every trade. The data can be sorted by "Strategy" to determine which strategy is giving better results by comparing the Reward to Risk Ratios.

Sometimes taking a screenshot of the charts with notes during entries and exits is useful. The screenshots help in analyzing the Trading Journal more effectively later.

TIP

Update the Trading Journal after every trade.

APPENDIX A: GLOSSARY

Ask Price – Lowest price a seller is willing to accept to sell his share.

Bear Market – Financial Markets with falling stock prices.

Beta – Measure of stocks' volatility compared to the General Market. General Market has a Beta of 1.0. If the individual stock swings more than the General Market over time, then the stock has a Beta above 1.0, and vice versa.

Bid Price – Highest price that a buyer is prepared to pay for a share.

Bid Ask Spread – Bid ask spread is the difference between the highest price that a buyer is willing to pay and the lowest price a seller is willing to accept.

Blue Chip – Refers to established, stable and well recognized companies. Blue chip stocks have a proven track record of profits and growth and are relatively safer investments.

Bull Market – Financial Markets with rising stock prices.

Buy – Buy shares of a company.

Buy and Hold – A passive investment strategy where an investor buys a stock and holds them for a longer period (few years to decades) regardless of market fluctuations.

Buy Limit Order – Buy Limit Order can only be executed at a Limit Price or lower.

Buy Stop Limit Order – It is a combination of 2 Orders: Stop Order and a Buy Limit Order. Once the Stop Price is reached, it becomes Limit Order to buy at Limit Price or better.

Day Order – A Buy or Sell Order that is only open until the end of the trading day.

Day Trading – Buying and selling stocks within the same trading day.

Discount Broker – A stockbroker who carries out buy and sell orders for their clients at reduced commissions (mostly through online platforms). They do not provide investment and research services for clients.

Dividend – A portion of the profit of a company paid to its shareholders.

Dollar Cost Average – A strategy to place a fixed dollar amount in an investment on a regular basis.

Float – Number of shares available for trading (Float = Shares Outstanding – Blocked shares – Restricted Shares).

Full-Service Broker – A licensed financial broker that provides wide variety of services, including research, facilitating trades, managing portfolios, retirement planning, and providing tax tips. Obviously, commissions are higher.

Good Till Cancel (GTC) Order – A Buy or Sell Order that remains active until either the Order is filled, or the Order is cancelled.

IPO – Initial Public Offering (IPO) or stock market launch is the process by which a private company goes public for the first time by selling shares of their company to investors.

Limit Order – An Order to buy or sell a stock at a specific price or better. Fills will not occur until the specific price or better has reached.

Liquidity – A situation where a trader can easily get in (buy) and get out (sell) of stocks.

Long Position – Trader buys a stock with the expectation that the stock price will rise.

Margin Account – An account where the Broker lends money to the account holder to buy stocks. The difference between the amount of the loan and the price of the stocks is called margin.

Market Cap – Total market value of a company's outstanding shares. Calculated by multiplying the current market price of a stock by company's outstanding shares.

Market Order – Market Orders guarantee immediate fills, but not the fill price. Therefore, fill prices when using Market Orders can be unfavorable.

Portfolio – A collection of investments (such as stocks) owned by an investor.

Position Trading – Trading style to capture gains in a stock with a longer holding time (few weeks to years).

Sell – Sell shares of a company.

Sell Limit Order – Sell Limit Order can only be executed at a limit price or higher.

Shares Outstanding – Total number of shares held by all its shareholders (including restricted shares and blocked shares).

Short Position – Trader sells a stock with the expectation that the stock price will decrease. Also called "Short Selling".

Stock Exchange – A facility where stockbrokers and traders can buy and sell securities such as shares of stocks, bonds, and other financial instruments.

Stop Loss Order – A limit or market order that automatically executes when the stock reaches a certain price.

Swing Trading – Trading style to capture gains in a stock over a period of few days to few weeks.

Trading Volume – Total number of shares traded between a buyer and a seller.

Trend – When the price is moving in one overall direction, either up or down.

Trend Trading – A trading style to capture gains of stock's momentum in a particular direction.

Volatility – A measurement on how fast a stock price is moving up or down.

Watchlist – A list of stocks being monitored for potential trading opportunities.

APPENDIX B: USEFUL WEBSITES

CHARTS

- https://www.tradingview.com/
- https://www.investing.com/charts/
- https://www.chartmill.com?affl=84995
- https://www.stockcharts.com

CHART PATTERNS

- https://school.stockcharts.com/doku.php?id=chart_analysis:chart_patterns
- https://www.investopedia.com/articles/technical/112601.asp
- https://www.investopedia.com/terms/a/ascendingtriangle.asp

COMPANY FINANCIALS

- https://www.morningstar.com
- https://www.quickfs.net

EARNINGS CALENDARS

- https://www.investing.com/earnings-calendar/
- https://finance.yahoo.com/calendar/earnings
- https://www.bloomberg.com/markets/earnings
  -calendar/us

ECONOMIC CALENDARS

- https://www.investing.com/economic-calendar/
- https://www.forexfactory.com/calendar.php
- https://www.dailyfx.com/economic-calendar

FINANCIAL WEBSITES

- https://finance.yahoo.com
- https://www.msn.com/en-us/money
- https://www.zacks.com
- https://www.fool.com
- https://www.google.com/finance
- https://www.msnbc.com
- https://www.cnbc.com
- https://money.cnn.com/data/markets/
- https://www.bloomberg.com

LEARNING

- https://school.stockcharts.com/doku.php?id=ch
  art_analysis:introduction_to_candlesticks

- https://school.stockcharts.com/doku.php?id=technical_indicators
- https://www.msn.com/en-us/money/investing/start-investing
- https://us.spindices.com/index-literacy/

STOCK SCREENERS

- https://finviz.com/?a=65820987 (go to "screener" tab)
- https://www.tradingview.com/
- https://www.chartmill.com?affl=84995
- https://finance.yahoo.com/screener/new
- https://www.msn.com/en-us/money/stockscreener/
- https://www.barchart.com/stocks/stocks-screener?viewName=filter_view
- https://www.investfly.com/screener/builder/
- https://www.screener.in

TECHNICAL ANALYSIS

- https://school.stockcharts.com/doku.php?id=technical_indicators
- https://simplywall.st/about
- https://stockinvest.us

WATCHLIST

- https://www.tradingview.com/

- https://www.investing.com/portfolio/
- https://www.msn.com/en-us/money/watchlist
- https://www.barchart.com/my/watchlist

WORLD INDICES

- https://www.tradingview.com/markets/indices/quotes-major/
- https://us.spindices.com
- https://www.investing.com/indices/world-indices

APPENDIX C: SUMMARY TABLE

CHAPTERS	YES/NO
1: Basics Internet Connection, Computer, Reasonable Capital, Brokerage Account, Charting Platform, Basic Knowledge.	
2: Overall Market Trend Stock Index: S&P 500 (SPX) Condition 1 (weekly chart) – 50 SMA is above 200 SMA	
3: Stocks Watchlist Create a "Watchlist" (all Index stocks) Highlight stocks which meet the following conditions: Condition 1 (weekly chart): Have smooth up trending pattern Condition 2 (weekly chart): 50 SMA is above 200 SMA Condition 3 (weekly chart): Price pattern shows higher highs and higher lows These stocks are:	

CHAPTERS	YES/NO
4: Leading Sectors and Stocks Leading Common Sectors (1w+1m+3m): Leading Common Sectors (1m+3m+6m): Leading Common Sectors (3m+6m+1y): Leading Common Sectors (6m+1y): Leading Stocks in Leading Sector 1: Leading Stocks in Leading Sector 2: Leading Stocks in Leading Sector 3:	
5: Money Management Stock Symbol: Account Risk: Trade Risk/Share (Stop Loss): Maximum Position Size:	
6: Trading Plan Stocks selected: Strategy: Minimum Reward to Risk Ratio: Entry Setup criteria:	

CHAPTERS	YES/NO
Trigger Price (Buy Price):	
Trade Risk/Share (Stop Loss):	
Initial Stop Loss Price:	
Plan to raise the Stop Loss:	
Profit Targets:	
Earnings: No Earnings release for these stocks in the next 30 days	
High Impact News: No high impact news coming up at the time of buying the stocks	
## 7: Trading Journal	
Trading Journal updated?	

APPENDIX D: FREE BONUS

Thank you for reading this book. As promised, you can download the following documents for FREE.

- Money Management Calculator,
- Trading Journal,
- Summary Table, and
- A PDF copy of all Figures and Tables.

Please click the link below for the above:

- https://www.thinkandretire.com/bonus-leading-stocks/

APPENDIX E: FURTHER RESEARCH

This book presents several ideas about identifying the overall market trends, leading sectors, leading stocks beating the broader market, relative strengths, money management techniques, stock scanning, calculating stop loss, and profit targets, amongst others. The traders can use these ideas and tools to develop their own strategies. The commonly used technical indicators and setups listed below may provide some guidance. The internet has many useful resources for references.

- Moving Average Crossovers
- MACD Divergence
- MACD crossovers
- 52-week high breakouts
- Parabolic SAR
- Bollinger Bands
- Commodity Channel Index
- Aroon Oscillator
- Improving Chaikin Money Flow (CMF)
- Keltner Channel Breakouts

- Price Action Setups
- Support and Resistance
- Gap Ups, and so on and forth

There are thousands of setups and indicators. I hope that the above list gives the readers some ideas for further research.

ABOUT THE AUTHOR

Thank you for taking the time to read this book. My name is Debabrata (David) Das, Ph.D. I have been trading since 1999. I am a DIY (Do It Yourself) Investor.

I worked as an engineer for 26 years before retiring in 2015. Now I am more focused on doing things that I enjoy the most.

Many people have asked me to share what steps I took to retire early. This book will help me share some of my personal trading experiences and knowledge that I have gained over the years. I am hoping that this knowledge may help others in their stock trading journey.

Please do write to me if you have any questions or comments by visiting www.thinkandretire.com and clicking the "Contact" button. I will personally respond to you.

If you have enjoyed the book and found it helpful, please leave a positive review on your favorite website(s). Thank you.

www.ingramcontent.com/pod-product-compliance
Lightning Source LLC
Chambersburg PA
CBHW070553220526
45467CB00003B/1203